HEALING AMERICA

Also by Richard Cornuelle:

RECLAIMING THE AMERICAN DREAM
DE-MANAGING AMERICA

HEALING AMERICA

AMERICA

Richard Cornuelle

G.P. Putnam's Sons
New York

The text of this book is set in 11 point Caledonia

Library of Congress Cataloging in Publication Data

Cornuelle, Richard C., date.
  Healing America.

    1. United States—Economic policy—1981–
  2. United States—Economic conditions—1971–
  3. Associations, institutions, etc.—United States.
  I. Title.
  HC106.8.C67 1983   338.973   82-24015
  ISBN 0-399-12785-2

      PRINTED IN THE UNITED STATES OF AMERICA

To my mother
1887–1982

Contents

1

The Great Misunderstanding

"The human tragedy is that a way of life becomes a way of
life when most people can conceive of no alternative."
                                              Harry Johnson

The Great Crash of 1929 and the Great Depression that continued through the thirties left a great legacy: a nearly universal belief that it is both proper and possible for government to
correct the deficiencies of an industrial economy and provide
stability and security—employment for those who can work
and a system of supports for those who can't. "What do the
American people want more than anything else?" Franklin
Roosevelt asked the Democratic Convention that had just
nominated him for president in 1932: "Work and security."

Now, a half a century later, government is clearly failing in
both these central ambitions. It has not produced stability. On
the contrary, policies designed to produce stable, full employment have become the principal causes of instability and unemployment. And far from creating security, public policy has
brought about a universal insecurity. The economy is stagnating as a result of policies designed to prevent stagnation. Something elemental has gone wrong. It is becoming clear that fifty
years of public policy were built on a false premise.

A great error is often a great truth that has been misunderstood and misapplied. It had become clear by the thirties that
industrialization had radically and permanently altered the
agenda of public business. In an industrial society, full employment had to be a common concern—a collective concern—
just as floods and famines and forest fires had been in an earlier

time. A civilized society could not let the full weight of a systemic, society-wide defect fall arbitrarily on a few of its members. A human community cannot employ a convenient fraction of its industrial work force and let the rest suffer or starve. It is morally intolerable. That was the great truth.

The great misunderstanding—the great *non sequitur* that gained credence in the 1930s—was that the state is the instrument through which this collective responsibility is best exercised.

During the fifty years that followed the Great Crash, there occurred a thorough transformation of American society—the progressive substitution of government programs for the decentralized network of institutions and practices through which Americans had acted on most of their common concerns for a hundred and fifty years. The state not only failed; it crowded out institutions that might have succeeded.

Before the Great Depression, there was a formidable alternative to government action on most public problems—health, foreign aid, civil rights, regulation, education. American society had become highly pluralistic. There was a widely shared assumption that the strength and conscience of the nation lay not in Washington, but in the vast variety of half-invisible, nongovernmental institutions and customs that were perhaps as complex as our language.

Before the Depression, the state was not society; it was only a specialized instrument of society, and the ideal of community was largely expressed in other ways. To say that Americans were enterprising and self-reliant—individualistic—is a gross understatement. The American sense of community, as most Old World observers attested—among them Tocqueville, Dickens, Lord Bryce, John Stuart Mill—was more highly developed than anywhere else in the world. It was, they said, the most distinctive feature of the American landscape.

By 1880, there were at least 800 independent organizations in Philadelphia alone. By World War I, the independent sector had already become so ubiquitous as to have become largely invisible: independent organizations were our major social institutions. In 1915, two foundations, Rockefeller and Carnegie, spent twice as much for education and social service as did the federal government. In 1917, the Red Cross set a goal of $100 million, fifty times what it had spent in the three previous years. It exceeded the goal and in 1918 nearly doubled it. After the war, the United War Work Campaign raised another $200 million "to prevent the period of demobilization from becoming a period of demoralization."

When the Depression struck, the independent sector had become so large and complex as to be literally indescribable in any reasonable space. Nor had anyone ever bothered to catalog its elements or estimate its total contribution to the general welfare. Even now, the organizations of the "independent" sector have yet to be counted and classified. In spite of a generation of demoralizing neglect, there are probably three-quarters of a million visible voluntary organizations in the United States, plus 7 million or more less formal ones acting on the public business in hundreds of ways—from running colleges and hospitals to disaster relief and suicide prevention.

There are the great businesslike giants in the field: Underwriters Laboratories, Blue Cross–Blue Shield, the American Arbitration Association, and the Teachers Insurance and Annuity Association. There is the Little People of America, an association of the nation's 100,000 dwarfs. There is an Association for the Study of Headache and a clearing house through which amputees can trade the odd left or right shoes or gloves they can't use.

But, after the first three winters of the Great Depression, public confidence in independent action was exhausted. In time, the nation concluded that the independent sector could not, congenitally, cope with an industrial society's central problems—and that government could.

For a century before 1929, the total cost of all levels of government had never exceeded 10% of national income, except during major wars. Federal spending was normally about a third of that; two-thirds was state and local. Fifty years after 1929, the total cost of federal, state, and local government was approaching half the national income, and the division had been upended. Now two-thirds of the vastly greater cost of government was federal, and only a third state and local. The structure of American society had been altered elementally.

The independent sector stopped growing; it became something of a joke. Its forms survived, and since the sixties a kind of tentative renaissance has begun, but for the better part of a half century, it was on ice. Its rustic therapies were believed to be suited only to an earlier, simpler time. It was a proud part of the past, with its barn raisings and quilting bees and Christmas baskets, but in an industrial society it was technologically obsolete. The independent sector seemed to have no future. It should putter about with trivial tasks or, even better, rest in peace.

Thus, the heritage of the thirties is a society badly out of balance—misshapen—its governmental sector overgrown and its capacity for concerted action outside government severely underdeveloped.

Today, there is a crisis of another sort. The state is failing at the very tasks that caused Americans to abandon the independent sector.

The eminent management theorist Peter Drucker wrote, "There is mounting evidence that government is big rather than strong; that it is fat and flabby rather than powerful; that it costs a great deal but does not achieve much . . . the greatest disappointment, the great letdown is the fiasco of the Welfare State."

And Elliot Richardson, former secretary of Health, Education and Welfare, delivered a disquieting valedictory as he left the department in 1973: "There is an increasingly pervasive sense not only of failure, but of futility . . . the legislative process has become a cruel shell game and the service system has become a bureaucratic maze—inefficient, incomprehensible and inaccessible." At that time the budget of the department was less than a third its present size.

In the sixties, another ominous complication began to attract attention. In 1930, Americans paid a dime for a loaf of bread, just as their grandfathers had done. For nearly two centuries, while prices sometimes rose and receded in war-related disturbances, the price level was basically flat. The price of a Model-T Ford *fell* from $850 in 1908 to $360 in 1927. But, beginning in 1939, prices began to rise relentlessly almost every year. A generation of Americans has come to accept inflation as a fact of life.

By 1960, prices were beginning to move in a great, sickening surge, in an inflation without precedent in modern U.S. history. By 1980, the dollar had lost two-thirds of its 1960 purchasing power. When prices in England increased by a factor of six over the 150 years from 1500 to 1650, historians called it the "price revolution." Our price level rose as much in forty years, a certain sign that the government's responsibilities were outgrowing its resources.

In the seventies, roughly on its bicentennial, the United States, for the first time since the Great Crash, began to regress economically. American society was beginning to sink under the weight of a government that was taking more than two-fifths of national income.

It was then that journalist Jude Wanniski and economist Arthur Laffer and other spokesmen for supply-side economics began a useful national teach-in on an ancient axiom: there are limits to a society's tolerance for taxation. Taxes that are too high and too close to the bone of the nation's productive capacity become self-defeating. In the United States, they said, taxes were already either driving tax producers underground or reducing their ability to pay taxes. Still higher tax rates would probably reduce tax revenues. At least in theory, lower tax rates might even produce greater tax revenues.

This recognition sharply reduced the nation's policy alternatives. Once the limits of taxation have been reached or exceeded, there are only two other ways government can pay its way: it can borrow from the public or it can borrow from itself. And each of these two methods has its own limits. Borrowing large amounts from the investment public crowds out private investment, pushes interest rates up, and thus asphyxiates the economy. When government borrows from itself, the Federal Reserve creates the money it "lends" to the Treasury, and this turning of debt into money is the primal cause of inflation.

All the policy alternatives are destructive. Like walking on hot sand, the policy emphasis shifts restlessly from taxation to borrowing to money creation, as the destructive effect of first one and then another becomes intolerable. This is demogogically translated in the popular debate as a "trade-off" between unemployment and inflation, and each is described by its opponents as a "cure" for the other.

Still, in the teeth of overwhelming evidence that government programs are not working and that their costs are becoming more and more destructive, government continues to grow, as the agenda of urgent, half-finished public business continues to mount. A third of the nation's families were victims of violent crime in 1981. In Coney Island, retired people can do their shopping safely only with a police escort. Unemployment among young blacks is twice as high as the highest national Depression rate. More and more students—some say as many as 60 million—have left school after a dozen years unable to read and write. Urban transportation systems are collapsing. The automobile industry and the steel industry are deathly sick.

And while government action is not a satisfactory way to cope with the public business, it is now the only way we know. So a number of incompatible perceptions have converged. Government programs work badly. They are costing more than we can afford. We need more of them.

2

This Self-Defeating Society

"The inflation of our time . . . is not just a disorder of the monetary system which can be left to financial experts to redress; it is a . . . disorder of society. [It] . . . belongs to the things which can be understood and remedied only in the area beyond supply and demand."

Wilhelm Röpke
A Humane Economy

Contemporary public opinion is, understandably, confused and contradictory. It can no longer be understood in terms of swings to and from the polarities of liberalism and conservatism. We are all liberals in the sense that we want to live in a workable, responsible society where the streets are clean and safe and the poor are decently cared for. And we are all conservatives at least in the sense that we do not want to see the country go broke.

The public's political views are not volatile, as some poll watchers have suggested; they have been consistently ambivalent for fifty years. Most people believe it is in the general interest to reduce the role of government; when the public superego speaks, it tells the pollsters that government is dangerously overgrown. But, as members of one or more of the hundreds of interlocking special interests, at the level of bread and butter and cold cash, the public speaks with another, louder voice and insists on increased government spending. These desires for larger benefits, taken together, form a much more specific and immediate impulse, and one much more readily translatable into political power. There is a large constituency for survival, but it is too diffuse to be politically effective.

For example, four out of five Americans believe government has become too powerful; 84% believe it spends too much money; 69% of the interviewees told *U.S. News & World Report* that government is the principal cause of inflation. But 72% favor more federal spending for crime prevention; 60%, more for defense; 57%, more for health; 55%, more for education; and 51%, more for the environment. Although 69% favor a constitutional amendment to limit federal deficits, half would withdraw their support if it meant cutting back their favorite federal programs—and every program is someone's favorite.

The disillusion, indecision, and worried ambivalence of the American electorate were clearly revealed in the 1980 election. There was no question who won, but there were some serious questions what that victory meant. When 22% of the eligible electorate voted for George McGovern for president in 1972, his showing was seen as a humiliating defeat. Then, in 1980, when 27% of the eligible electorate voted for Ronald Reagan, we were told we had been witness to at least a "massive mandate" and perhaps even "the end of an era." *The New York Times'* Anthony Lewis called it a "profound and general turn to conservatism."

But the large meaning suggested by the one-sided electoral vote was partly illusory, for the number of eligible voters who chose not to vote had increased again as it has in every presidential election for twenty years. The United States now has a lower rate of political participation than any democratic country except Botswana. (Democracy seems most robust in Sierra Leone where, in 1977, the turnout was a stunning 103%.)

If the 1980 results are rearranged as percentages of the potential vote, the picture blurs: Reagan 26.7%, Carter 21.4%, others 4.2%—and 47.7% abstaining. About one potential voter in four preferred Mr. Reagan to Mr. Carter. About one in five would have preferred Mr. Carter to Mr. Reagan. Nearly half expressed no preference. This was of course a decisive result, but a marginally significant one. It means only that the ambivalence that has shaped American politics for a full half century now seems more acute than ever.

There is unquestionably a troubled conservative tide running in the land, as it has for years. But the more familiar liberal tide is still running too.

Governor Reagan simply mirrored this abiding ambivalence without even pretending to resolve it. He promised to cut government in general without cutting anything in particular. And because he is a likable man who expressed this soothing *non sequitur* with an engaging, bashful sincerity that somehow made it seem legitimate, almost 27% of the people voted for him. But that is surely something less than a "profound and general turn to conservatism."

Reagan's program, characterized as a revolution, proposed not to cut government (there were a few exceptions) but to reduce its rate of growth somewhat. Carter's lame duck budgets had proposed increasing federal spending about 13% a year for three years. The Reagan administration proposed reducing that rate to about 5%. The Reaganites spoke of a "hemorrhaging" federal budget, but promised not to touch the parts that were hemorrhaging. Using a time-tested Potomac euphemism, they called these categories "uncontrollable."

But even the Reagan plan to reduce the rate of governmental growth somewhat elicited anguished protests from every affected quarter of American society, from tobacco growers to social scientists to social security recipients. "How can you be so cruel?" demanded one senator. "Thousands of elderly citizens . . . are literally eating out of garbage cans to stay alive." Taken together, these protesters were saying that an $800 billion federal budget—which could probably be financed only by currency inflation—was not enough.

By the end of his first hundred days, Reagan had spent his meager political capital in pursuit of a minimal, if not inconsequential, ambition, and some of his conservative critics were saying that he had misunderstood his mandate. It is more likely that he understood it perfectly. But in the off-year election of 1982, which was supposed to "solidify the emerging Republican majority," the president's party lost twenty-four House seats, the worst setback for a president since 1950.

Public policy has come to a dead end. Essential social goals are in collision. We cannot make society habitable without making government bigger. And paying the costs of bigger government causes problems—unemployment and inflation—which add further to the cost of government. Government is growing as it fails, and, to a chilling degree, it is growing because it fails.

In the past, we became accustomed to making difficult public choices; now we confront choices that are literally impossible—choices between order and survival, between humanity and solvency. We have become, as Lester Thurow put it, a zero-sum society, a self-defeating society, a society that cannot attain one goal without compromising another. Paul Johnson, former editor of Britain's *New Statesman,* has written that big government "is taking us along a road toward a divided and querulous society in which everyone pursues rights and no one accepts duties. In both our countries [England and the United States] government agencies encourage a maximist attitude to rights—that they must be exacted always, to the limit, and regardless of the cost to the community." He is describing a society that has turned its energy against itself. The extent of the programs to which people believe themselves entitled is no longer negotiable, even if the price is the destruction of our society's ability to provide them.

Our society is showing signs of enormous strain, if not disintegration. Ours is called the "me" generation. "For God's sake," begs a national columnist, "give me something to be enthusiastic about!" Social theory has become pessimistic, concerned with limits and how to live with them.

Most alarming is the immense and growing popularity of an apocalyptic economics that predicts the breakdown of the system and peddles intricate, half-mad "survival strategies." These people claim that America is finished as a workable human community—that it is time for every man to look out for himself. The widespread popularity of this nonsense is a saddening measure both of the level of anxiety among us and the degree to which our once proud sense of community has eroded.

The American government is losing its capacity to govern. As the Congress has tried vainly to manage thousands of unmanageable programs, its attention to essentials has been distracted and dissipated. There is a dangerous decline of intelligent, democratic control of foreign policy and defense. We look primarily to government to keep the peace—but increasingly there is no peace.

The nation continues on the course charted in the thirties, despite the fact that events have largely discredited the cosmology on which it was based, as scholars have reconsidered more coolly the presuppositions of that terror-stricken era.

The most damaging intellectual legacy of the Depression is not economic but social: the assumption that nongovernmental institutions are unable to cope with the collective problems of an industrial society. This premise became a self-fulfilling prophesy and has left American society badly disfigured.

Now, a half century after the coming of the New Deal, it is time to review the factual and emotional circumstances that led us to conclude that the state could produce stability and that the independent sector could not. It is time to ask if we can rebuild a vigorous independent sector; whether there can be a sustained, concerted, national effort to create an independent alternative to the ruins of the welfare state; whether we can rethink and redefine the public business for today's collective agenda and invent ways to act on it decisively.

The obstacles are immense.

The headlong substitution of state for community has demoralized the nation's nongovernmental institutions, aborted their development, and retarded social innovation for the last half century. The leaders of the independent sector have been conditioned by decades of neglect to think in small terms about the sector's possibilities. Government has consciously pre-empted the resources that might have nourished the independent sector. Thousands of voluntary agencies, tired of living on leftovers, have turned to Washington for support and have thus become, in effect, agents of the state.

The nation has become economics-obsessed and politics-obsessed, and has pushed these disciplines far beyond their limits. And, today, America suffers from a sickness that economic analysis cannot clarify and political action cannot cure. Having come perilously close to viewing society and state as identical, we are trying vainly to force economics and politics to do the work of elemental social reform.

As government has increasingly monopolized the public business, the role of the citizen has been dangerously diminished. Citizenship once meant more than voting—it meant direct, personal, hands-on involvement in the common concerns of the community. Today, that livelier dimension has nearly disappeared, and it has been reduced to a matter of picketing and petitioning the state. Americans can scarcely imagine basic social reform *outside the political process.*

3

The Rise and Fall of the Independent Sector

"The question is whether our beautiful, libertarian, pluralist and populist experiment is viable in modern conditions."

Paul Goodman
People or Personnel

Any society searches eternally for the right distribution of responsibility among its institutions. The process is complex and continuous, if not necessarily wise or just or effective. It is influenced by a thousand factors of chance, custom, superstition, and prejudice. Sometimes the process is contrived; sometimes it is spontaneous, but somehow or other the public business gets defined and assigned and redefined and reassigned. It happens when Congress passes a law or aldermen an ordinance or when people give blood or money or advice. It goes on whenever an improvement committee or a posse or a lynch mob is formed.

Some of the forces at work in the process pull responsibility toward the center; other forces pull it away. The events of the thirties altered this institutional balance profoundly, reinforcing American society's propensity to centralize. The first casualty of the Depression Era was the tradition of acting on the public business outside of government that had roots in the colonial past.

America's voluntary tradition was apparently not imported; the colonists organized their communities according to the conventional political wisdom of the Old World. In the beginning this amounted to a kind of theocratic, backwoods, municipal socialism.

Local government assumed nearly total responsibility for the conduct of the public business. Towns, then as now, built roads and bridges, schools of sorts, and helped the poor. But the town also hired the preacher, built the meeting house he preached in, and punished anyone who came late. The town controlled the location of its tanneries and regulated the quality of its bread. If a citizen was thought to be wasting too much time in the taverns, the selectmen ordered the innkeepers to keep him out.

Colonial America was at first much more monolithic than pluralistic. But rigid Old World organization was ill-suited to the task of surviving in what has been called a "howling wilderness." After one particularly terrifying season, William Bradford, governor of Plymouth Colony, said flatly, "Martial Law did not grow corn."

There was often no alternative to freer forms of independent mutual action even if it violated ancient prejudices about how things got done. There were no police to call, no troops to summon. Anyone who waited for the troops, someone said, didn't last long.

So, in colonial America, voluntary action began to develop in unprecedented ways. Groups were formed for every imaginable purpose: to help widows and orphans, immigrants and blacks, debtors and prisoners, old women and young prostitutes; to promote morality, temperance, thrift, and industrious habits; to educate poor children in free schools; to reform gamblers, drunkards, and juvenile delinquents.

In 1774, Philadelphia physicians formed the Society for Inoculating the Poor Gratis. In Boston, citizens created the Society for Encouraging Industry and Employing the Poor. In almost every colony, societies to aid disabled seamen were set up. South Carolinians formed a society to relieve "every poor person without distinction."

Some of these early voluntary efforts were silly and self-righteous. Some were highly controversial. Some involved a handful of people and, even then, some involved thousands. Some were formed to solve imaginary problems. Two societies in Boston and Philadelphia were set up to aid the victims of "suspended animation"—people who seemed to be dead but really were not. Since drowning was the most common apparent cause of this condition, the societies maintained caches of special equipment at waterfront taverns—bellows for inflating the lungs and fumigators for pumping tobacco smoke into suspected victims.

But later events proved that this historic stirring of voluntary action was only a bare beginning. The Revolution itself, and particularly the unusual way the colonists conducted it, seemed to reinforce the voluntary tradition.

The Americans fought the Revolution with an amateur army. Almost every colonist owned a musket, a circumstance European governments of the time would never have tolerated and which colonial governors found unnerving. Virginia's Governor Sir William Berkeley complained bitterly of the special hazards of governing a people of whom six out of seven are "Poore, Endebted, Discontented and Armed."

The American Militia was a citizen army that has been described as "a band of casually gathered, haphazardly-armed amateurs, over whom there was no effective central command." The officers were usually elected.

Responsibility was widely diffused. One reason the American Army proved hard to defeat was that it was not really an army. It had no center; "its center," an analyst said, "was everywhere." And the idea of dispersed responsibility apparently carried over into the realm of social organization.

In Concord, where the war had begun, the townspeople discovered what a historian called "the secret of voluntary association." A Fire Society was formed to put out Concord's fires. An anonymous music lover formed a Harmonic Society to improve the quality of singing in Concord's churches. "Build your own world," Emerson had admonished New Englanders,

and by the turn of the century, in Concord and other towns
throughout the new nation, the people had put in place a "rich
network of self-help groups." When the political revolution
was over, an ongoing revolution of another sort began.

By the time Alexis de Tocqueville came to America in 1831,
Americans had begun to build a society with three strong sectors—the governmental, the commercial, and the independent—all based on a principle of broad participation.

Tocqueville was the first to report the extraordinary growth
of independent action, even into fields thought properly governmental, and to recognize its significance.

"Anyone," he wrote to a friend in Paris, "is free to found a
public school and to direct it as he pleases . . . the consumers
being the judges and the state taking no hand whatever. . . ."
And before compulsory tax-supported education became universal in the mid-1850s, the independent sector had set up and
operated hundreds of private academies and so-called "charity
schools."

At the same time, the sector put in place a remarkable national network of colleges and universities; Harvard was the
first, established in 1636. By 1880, England, with a population
of 23 million, supported four degree-granting institutions.
Ohio, with a population of 3 million, had thirty-seven.

The activities of the voluntary sector had even then become
too vast and varied to catalog. William Ellery Channing re-
marked that it was hard to find a good or bad cause for which
an association had not been formed. The sector financed and
popularized polar expeditions, fostered an explosion of scientific inquiry, and promoted the Washington Monument. Ame-
lia Bloomer launched her campaign for sensible women's
clothes. Societies were formed to provide reading glasses for
old people, homes for fallen and repentant women, and to help
young brides set up housekeeping. There was a Society for the
Observance of the Seventh Commandment, a Society for Promoting Manual Training in Literary Institutions, and a Society
for Alleviating the Miseries of Public Prisons.

The sector's concerns, even then, were international. In 1832, when an American ship arrived at the famine-stricken Cape Verde Islands, some of the starving inhabitants rowed out, hoping to buy something to eat from the ship's stores. They found that Americans had sent the whole ship, laden with food and supplies, to help them.

One independent organization, the American Colonization Society, formed in 1817, raised money, bought land in Africa, and established Liberia.

Beginning in 1853, New York City's Children's Aid Society sent homeless children—over the years nearly 100,000 of them—on "orphan trains" from the "vileness" of New York's streets to "wholesome" farm families in the Middle West.

The emancipation of the nation's slaves was itself a result of over a century of sustained effort by hundreds of independent organizations involving hundreds of thousands of persons, both black and white.

During the Civil War, the U.S. Sanitary Commission combined the efforts of thousands of local organizations to make conditions in army camps and hospitals less often lethal. John Stuart Mill commented: "History afforded no other example of so great a work of usefulness extemporized by the spontaneous self-devotion and organizing genius of a people altogether independent of the government."

As the United States expanded and new problems appeared, the sector invented new methods of common action, often stunning in their scope and originality. The great cooperative roundups in the West were necessary not just to gather cattle for shipment but to sort out their ownership. Branding was an essential social invention for the particular requirements of the Great Plains—a portable proof of ownership.

The pond freshet was another wonderfully ingenious community enterprise—a way to move freight down streams normally too small to be navigable. A carefully organized pond freshet could produce an artificial rush of water just long enough to float freight downstream. The principal branches of the creek—sometimes dozens of them—were dammed in a way that permitted quick release. Then, according to a meticulous schedule, the pools of water were let go, one by one, to create a great temporary rush of water. The boatmen, according to a contemporary account, "stand ready to loose their lines. A cool pushing breeze is the first sign ... and soon after comes the swirling waters." A single freshet, after weeks of preparation involving hundreds of persons, might carry hundreds of freight-laden boats downstream.

In those early years, what came to be called the American dream was being realized—a society that was at once free, prosperous, and caring. The pursuit of each of these ideals supported the others. Americans were free because the power of the government was limited. They were prosperous because they were free. And because they applied the fruits of that prosperity—time and money—to solving their common problems, the need for government was limited and Americans remained free.

The coming of the industrial revolution altered the agenda of these common concerns suddenly and radically.

The social transformation that took place in the United States in the years between the Civil War and the Great Crash in 1929 was without precedent in history. Before the Civil War, most Americans were farmers, using, for the most part, implements that would have been familiar to the Babylonians. Within a single generation, most American breadwinners were working for wages in offices and factories.

The American version of the industrial revolution was even more abrupt and wrenching than its European predecessor, which was far advanced when ours began in earnest. The American colonies had been flatly forbidden to participate in Europe's industrial revolution and, according to legend, the know-how that formed the basis for America's textile industry had to be bootlegged from England. This enforced postponement proved beneficial in a backhanded way. It meant that the industrialization of America, when it came, was based on a newer, more efficient generation of technology. Europe's factories were powered by moving water and by steam. America's industrial revolution, after Gramme's invention of the dynamo in 1872, was driven by electricity. It was to be a vital difference.

The suddenness and scale of the transfiguration was illustrated by steel. In 1870, America had no steel industry or nearly none. We bought steel and iron in Europe. Twenty years later we were the world's major steel producer, turning out a third of the world's supply.

A Pennsylvania mill, founded in 1867, made 1005 tons of steel in its first year. Ten years later that one mill was outproducing Russia, Belgium, and Sweden combined. What was a small, local textile mill in Manchester, New Hampshire, before the Civil War, began, after the war, to produce fabric a yard wide at the rate of a mile a minute.

Suddenly, the independent sector's forms lost their relevance, and America's fabled sense of community had to find new forms appropriate to new and unfamiliar tasks. A sector of society whose therapies had been largely personal and local faced problems that were more systemic and general.

The agenda of common concerns in a pre-industrial society had been long and complex: fire protection, education, care of the disabled and indigent, the promotion of scientific research, the prevention and treatment of real and sometimes imagined diseases, among many others.

But industrialization brought problems of a different order. Epidemic and famine were familiar, but large-scale unemployment was not. The idea of "retiring" from a family farm would have been thought peculiar. There had never before been a need to develop ways to keep capitalists from polluting the streams or watering their stock or peddling poisonous merchandise.

The industrial revolution meant that the idea of community had to be enlarged and extended to include national problems. Americans were not, apparently, dismayed by this new necessity. Historian Joan Hoff Wilson writes of the period between 1900 and 1914, "most middle class citizens remained convinced ... that they had the power and the time to effect a new social order."

In the early stages of America's industrial revolution, factory wages only supplemented what families produced on their farms, and continuity of employment was not so important. But as industrialization picked up speed and more and more people left the land for full-time factory work, they became totally dependent on their wages. That the principal social problem was now unemployment was widely acknowledged. Between the Civil War and the Crash, half the nation's farmers left their land, most of them in Mr. Ford's Model-Ts, to work in factories. There was a perennial proposal during economic slowdowns to permit the unemployed to farm the vacant lots in the nation's cities. Henry Ford himself told *Business Week:* "These great plants which gather perhaps 125,000 families around them, absolutely helpless except for one factory ... are wrong. Industry must de-centralize. It must break up into small plants in small towns and villages, where the workman can have a piece of ground and make himself sure of subsistence at least."

To lose one's job was no longer an inconvenience; it was an elemental human catastrophe. It was more than losing a crop; it was like losing the farm.

So working people everywhere felt deep in their bones a horror of unemployment and feared and despised a system that could deprive them of work without warning. Wage earners have sometimes resisted industrialization with a life-and-death ferocity. In 1811 mobs of Luddites wearing masks smashed stocking and lacemaking machines in Nottingham and burned down the houses of the men who owned them. In the 1820s, French finishers kicked machines to pieces with their wooden shoes. The impact of unemployment on the psyche is of course profound. Freud believed a man's job was his most important link with reality. When unemployment goes up, so do arrests, heart attacks, and commitments to mental institutions.

The Social Darwinists of the time contended (correctly) that recessions tended to correct themselves; that they were divinely ordained and should not be meddled with by any means. But they ignored the dreadful human consequences.

But most Americans acknowledged that unemployment was a community responsibility and sought voluntary solutions on a broad front. There were a number of experiments with unemployment insurance, but the principal emphasis was on the prevention of the business cycle, smoothing out its ups and downs—"regularizing" employment.

Firms searched for ways to stabilize demand with stepped-up selling efforts and price concessions in slack times, or by smoothing out production patterns by regulating inventory, or gearing capital improvements to the rise and fall of the cycle.

Henry S. Dennison, a Massachusetts paper manufacturer, introduced an elaborate stabilization program after the 1908 recession and publicized it widely. After the 1914 recession, Dennison added a program of countercyclical plant construction. In 1916 he introduced the nation's first unemployment insurance fund.

William G. Procter, president of Procter and Gamble, guaranteed his 5000 employees forty-eight weeks of work a year, as one part of a complex regularization program.

As early as 1914, reformers had a clear vision of a macroeconomic result achieved by microeconomic action—of voluntary stabilization of employment through coordinated action by businessmen, social scientists, local government officials, and management engineers.

There was an early recognition that facts about the larger economic picture would be a central resource, and between 1916 and 1920, a number of important independent economic research agencies were established—the National Bureau of Economic Research, the National Industrial Conference Board, the Brookings Institution, and the National Planning Association, among them.

By the 1920s, the progressive movement had developed two overlapping branches, unified by their conviction that an industrial society had new common responsibilities, but differing in their evolving views of which institutions should do what. The war had revived interest in a government-directed capitalism—corporatism—first proposed in the 1830s by Eugene Buret.

But the principal movement of the period was a nationwide effort outside government to stabilize employment by independent action. By 1920, 2000 business associations had been formed. Nearly a hundred engineering societies formed the Federated American Engineering Societies to work on irregular employment, which they saw as the central social problem. The movement was put to the test in the steep recession of 1921.

There were no reliable figures then, but unemployment rose sharply, probably to 3 to 5 million. Herbert Hoover, then secretary of commerce, had already become an international symbol of the helping hand—a Hercules of relief; in Finland, to "hoover" still means to help, and Marxist Maxim Gorki once said Hoover had saved 9 million Russian lives.

Hoover proposed a national Unemployment Conference to President Warren Harding on August 12, 1921, and in two weeks a planning committee had been assembled, including businessmen like Dennison and lions of labor like Samuel Gompers and John L. Lewis. Two weeks later the larger conference met. Harding told the conferees it was "inconceivable" that the United States "could allow any suffering amongst those of our people who desire to work."

The purpose of the conference, Hoover said, was to "mobilize local and private groups to act with a national purpose." Among other measures, the conference sought to establish an emergency unemployment committee in each of the 327 cities with more than 20,000 population. In two weeks, 209 committees had been formed. In Portland, Oregon, unemployed migrants were housed in vacant steelyards. In Detroit a campaign for odd jobs produced a thousand. In Waterloo, Iowa, workers put up 1 percent of their wages for relief. Buffalo raised $70,000 for a special relief fund; Kansas City raised $290,000. Free employment agencies were set up. Philadelphia's Holy Trinity Church set up an employment bureau free to anyone who agreed to attend a Bible class. Cities were encouraged to speed up construction plans.

The conference was an example of Hoover's developing vision of decentralized voluntary action in a nationally established framework—*concerted* but voluntary action. He sought to "mobilize the intelligence of the country, that the entire community may be instructed as to the part they may play in the effecting . . . of solutions." By spring 1922, the crisis had lessened, perhaps in part as a result of the efforts of the conference.

Efforts to predict and prevent business cycles continued through the twenties. Seasonal cycles were most predictable and susceptible to regularization. As the research centers developed better statistics, longer cycles could be forecast and corrected for: "A long view of business rather than a short view will enable firms to make headway toward stabilization."

An American Construction Council was formed in 1922 because building was so basic to the business cycle. It published weekly forecasts of construction conditions as guides for ironing out the fluctuations in 1923. Its chairman was Franklin D. Roosevelt.

In 1927, the great flood of the Mississippi left one and a half million people homeless in seven states. Within a few days, $17 million was raised, most of it by history's first nationwide radio appeal; 150 "great towns of tents" were set up, all by local committees of volunteers. Although the damage to crops and buildings was a staggering $300 million, the credit pools set up for replanting and rebuilding were overwhelmingly private and independent.

Voluntary stabilization methods based on increasingly accurate statistics seemed to pass the test of the 1927 recession. By then, about a third of the nation's employers were using some sort of stabilization device. Economist Sumner Slichter predicted that unemployment would soon disappear as employers became aware of its costs and worked out ways to prevent it.

Two years later the American economy collapsed in what came to be known as the Great Crash.

4

Our Great Depression

"It may be that the race is not always to the swift, nor the battle to the strong—but that's the way to bet. Nothing between humans is one to three. In fact, I long ago came to the conclusion that all life is six to five against."

Damon Runyon

On September 3, 1929, the Dow Jones average peaked at 381.17. Not for twenty-five years would it reach that level again.

Earlier that year, Irving Fisher, then the nation's best-known economist, had said we had reached a permanent high plateau.

The Crash, when it came, was not a single shock but a crushing series of shocks. The first sickening slide was Black Thursday—October 24, 1929. Then came Black Tuesday—October 29. And then for a while every day was black. Some investors cried uncontrollably; others kicked the tickers. A few (but not nearly so many as legend suggests) went up to the roof and jumped. But the collapse of the stock market was just the beginning.

After a year, *Business Week* was still insisting that business was suffering from a mild recession—"statistical sciatica"—and condemned the "blue funk brigades of business" who liked to take "June walks in the cemetery." But in time it was clear to everyone that something dreadful had happened to the American economy.

The bottom of the Depression, when we finally reached it, was terrifying. Hoover called it an "enormous wound," and

Roosevelt spoke of our "descent into economic hell." Between 1929 and early 1933:

- GNP had fallen by half;
- Corporate profits had fallen two-thirds;
- Nearly half the nation's factories had shut down;
- The stocks in the Dow Jones industrial average had lost four-fifths of their value;
- 5000 banks, about a third of the total, had closed their doors;
- Fifteen million people had lost their jobs;
- Almost a million families had lost their homes;

According to Harry Hopkins, 18 million Americans were on relief—in some counties 90% of the population.

The Great Depression was a national mortification. Men rode the subways all night to keep warm. Hobos and bindle-stiffs roamed the country in freight cars. People put IOUs in church collection plates. Illinois Wesleyan accepted vegetables for tuition.

Once-prosperous professionals sold shoe polish and flypaper door to door. The International Apple Shippers offered apples on credit to anyone who wanted to sell them, and college graduates peddled apples in the street in their caps and gowns.

For the first time in our history, more people left the United States than entered. When the Soviet Union advertised for 6000 skilled workers, 100,000 Americans applied.

The history of that era has over the years been reshaped into a folkloric melodrama. In the first act, President Hoover sits alone in the White House, eating seven-course dinners while the country goes to hell. (It is true, apparently, that all Hoover's butlers and footmen were exactly the same height, were forbidden to speak in the pantry, and were carefully taught not to let the silver strike the china when they were clearing away.)

Actually, Hoover's was not a passive presidency but a hyperactive one. To a degree obscured by time, Hoover, for better or worse, saw the presidency primarily as a platform for mobilizing voluntary action.

He began to act, confidently at first, as he had so often before, to organize a mass movement to deal with this new catastrophe.

The central problem was to stabilize employment until the fallen economy recovered. Relief had a lesser, temporary importance. There was as yet no national consensus on the desirability of unemployment insurance. William Green, head of the AFL, for example, thought it demoralizing and destructive. "The real remedy for unemployment," he said, "is employment."

Nor had retirement income yet become a priority concern. In 1930, 6.5 million Americans were over sixty-five, but almost all of them were supported by their families. Pensions were a novelty; fewer than 100,000 people had any kind of pension. About an equal number lived in locally supported "poorhouses" or on "poor farms."

Hoover had a highly specific intention: to stretch the half-developed resources of the independent sector—he called it "voluntary cooperation"—in the service of this new national emergency. "It is in the further development of this cooperation," he wrote, "and a sense of its responsibility that we should find solutions for many of our complex problems, and not by the extension of government into our economic and social life. The greatest function of government is to build up that cooperation and its most resolute action should be to deny the extension of bureaucracy."

Hoover's calls for stabilization in the early Depression years now seem ingenuous. But at the time he was appealing to a well-defined, rapidly developing movement which had apparently stood the test of the decade's earlier recessions and could reasonably be expected to work in 1929.

Hoover called wave after wave of businessmen to the White House and persuaded them to keep wages up despite plummeting prices, and to spread the work among all their employees instead of firing some. And business went into the red $3 billion to do it. He ordered the first door-to-door head count of the unemployed. He set up 3000 local committees to watch over state and local relief and promised to unlock the federal treasury wherever local money ran out. He set up the Federal Farm Board to stabilize farm prices by federal buying.

Businesses, big and little, tried at first to ride out the Depression, to keep their people on their payrolls until the storm was over. *Business Week* reported that for months business kept 12% more workers than it needed. U.S. Steel, Bethlehem, and Jersey Standard pledged to drop no employees and to pro-rate the work. Fourteen Rochester employers joined in a voluntary, noncontributory unemployment insurance plan. Forty Muskegan manufacturers pledged to reduce the work week to three days "until they had increased their working force to its normal size." B. F. Goodrich bought 275 acres for a community garden for part-time and former employees.

In 1931, the Red Cross turned down a proposed congressional grant of $25 million to help drought victims, choosing instead to raise the money. "All we pray for is that you [Congress] let us alone and let us do the job," said the chairman of the Red Cross central committee.

In Seattle, the figures for the Community Fund outlined the national experience. Money raised increased from $190,000 in 1929 to $304,000 in 1931. In the grim fiscal year that ended on September 30, 1932, the effort quadrupled to $1,221,000. (In 1933, when the federal government greatly expanded its effort, the Seattle Fund collapsed to $199,000, only a little more than its 1929 level.)

The first two winters of the Great Depression were grim, but Americans survived. Historians are still puzzled by the fact that health statistics improved—mortality rates declined perceptibly, and infant mortality dropped substantially. After the second winter, some cities discontinued relief.

But the worst was still waiting to unfold. In 1931, Europe's banks began to wobble. The Bank of England suspended gold payments. Hoover continued his efforts to mobilize voluntary action with an awesome tenacity. In October, he made his last effort to shore up the nation's crumbling credit structure by voluntary means. He proposed that bankers and businessmen form a National Credit Corporation with a capital of $500 million. But NCC failed to assemble the money it needed, and Hoover recommended the establishment of a federally financed Reconstruction Finance Corporation. "Thus," writes Joan Hoff Wilson, "the ill-fated Hoover administration became the first in American history to use the power of the federal government to intervene directly in the economy in time of peace." Labor leaders called RFC the big business breadline; *Business Week* called it, without irony, "the most advanced example of state capitalism outside of Italy and Russia."

But the devastation continued. In the end, mobs of frightened depositors stormed the windows of America's banks, and the Hoover administration ended with the worst bank panic in U.S. history. We were, Hoover said, "at the end of our string." His effort to use the White House as a bully pulpit to promote a voluntary solution to economic collapse had failed.

The strength and spirit of the independent sector were broken. Its half-finished efforts to achieve stabilization outside government, tested in the hurricane, had proved unequal to the task. Its plans to provide unemployment insurance were still tentative and experimental. It had scarcely acknowledged the need for retirement security in a society that had so recently begun to retire in significant numbers.

Hoover's reputation was swept away in the wreckage as the hatred of terrified and demoralized people was directed against him, the living symbol of a lost faith. The nightclub jokes were merciless. In one, Hoover asks his secretary of the treasury for a nickel to phone a friend. "Here's a dime," says Mellon. "Phone them both."

When he went home to San Francisco to vote, a jeering crowd strewed stink bombs in his path. After his defeat at the polls, a member of his own party formally proposed his impeachment.

In the mythic version of the thirties drama, President Roosevelt drives the insensitive and indifferent Hoover from the

White House, scorns Hoover's finicky hesitation to put the full powers of government to work for recovery, reassures the people with a fireside chat or two, launches the New Deal, and cures the Depression.

The truth was so much more complicated and contradictory that we are still only beginning to sort it out. To begin with, Roosevelt shared with Hoover the prevailing preference for voluntary action. "The first principle I would lay down," he told a campaign audience in 1932, "is that the primary duty rests on the community, through local government and private agencies, to take care of the relief of unemployment."

In 1930, he had asked, "Is there any possible device to be worked out along volunteer lines by which the total wheat acreage of the nation could gradually be decreased?"

And in his relief message of March 1936, Roosevelt told business he was asking for a less-than-expected level of relief "on condition, however, that private employers hire many of those on relief rolls." And in a half-forgotten plea to business to take the responsibility for full employment, he continued, "Frankly, there is little evidence that large and small employers by individual and uncoordinated action can absorb large numbers of new employees. A vigorous effort on a national scale is necessary by voluntary, concerted action of private industry."

Roosevelt's 1932 platform had promised to roll back Hoover's impulsive and misguided state socialism, which was only making matters worse, cut spending, set enterprise free so it could get moving again, and above all keep the dollar sound and the destructive power of the government contained. The campaigning Roosevelt sounded so much like the supply-side economists of today that Ronald Reagan could not resist quoting him in his Detroit acceptance speech forty-eight years later.

But as soon as Roosevelt took office, a woman in Chicago complained she had to buy all the hourly editions of the afternoon papers to keep up with the president. He was the personification of political activism. "Above all," he once said, "try something. If it works, we'll do it some more. If it doesn't work, we'll try something else."

Roosevelt had been crippled by polio and walked with braces. Someone once asked him how he could make so many momentous decisions with such a light heart. "If you had spent years . . . in bed trying to wiggle your big toe," he said, "these decisions might not seem so momentous to you."

When visitors came to Washington for Roosevelt's inauguration, there was no place to cash a check. "What do I predict?" financier Eugene Grace told reporters. "I predict no more. Let us rather go uptown to the Cathedral and pray." By 1933, in Buffalo, more than half the unemployed had had no work for a year, and a third had had none for two years.

Roosevelt gathered his famous brains trust around him and went to work for recovery: Rexford Tugwell, Raymond Moley, Felix Frankfurter, Donald Richberg, Isador Lubin, and dozens more. "It is time," he had written in 1931, "for the country to become fairly radical for at least one generation."

"We didn't admit it at the time," Tugwell said forty years later, "but practically the whole New Deal was extrapolated from programs that Hoover started."

It is sometimes said that America was close to revolution during the depths of the Great Depression. But scholars who have studied unemployment more carefully find that, far from galvanizing people to violent action, it reduces them to frightened impotence. Historian John Garraty writes that jobless protests were "sporadic, unfocused and . . . merely rhetorical." A contemporary reporter described the famous 1932 bonus marchers as "the army of bewilderment," whose members behaved with "a curious melancholy." Another reporter, after crisscrossing the country in a car for seven months, was above all outraged by the unemployed workers' "passive acceptance of their condition."

A sociologist called the unemployed he studied "scattered, loose, perplexed and hopeless . . . a mass numerically, but not

socially." Three times as many U.S. workers voted for the
Communist candidate in 1912 as in 1932. Americans were,
capitalists and workers together, above all desperately afraid.

First Roosevelt declared his "bank holiday." He forbade
anyone to send money out of the country. Congress, it was
said, passed the bills Roosevelt sent up without reading
them—and maybe that's true.

He called in gold and made it a crime to hold it. Then, in a
complicated amendment to a farm relief bill, the United States
put a floating price on gold and devalued the dollar by half.
When the dust settled, Americans could trade their money for
other paper money but not for gold.

Opposition was simply pushed out of the way. Thomas P.
Gore, the scholarly, blind Senator from Oklahoma, who compared the gold measure to the "total depravity" of Henry VIII,
was purged from the Senate in 1936.

Although hardly anyone noticed it, and although these measures were called "temporary," it was the end of one era and
the beginning of another. Henceforth our currency would be
managed by a central authority. Two centuries of economic
thought were put aside, not as a result of a long, orderly process of reappraisal, but as a desperate, ad hoc response to be-
wildering immediacies. The rationalization came much later.

When, after devaluation, gold prices didn't respond rapidly
enough, the United States went into the world gold market.
Treasury Secretary Henry Morgenthau went to Roosevelt's
bedroom every morning and sat on the edge of his bed while
together they decided on the price of gold. "If anyone ever
knew," Morgenthau wrote in his diary, "how we set the gold
price through a combination of lucky numbers and the like, I
think they would be really frightened."

The closest thing to a theory behind the Roosevelt New
Deal was the same plausible diagnosis of the cause of the continuing Depression heard in the barbershops and pool halls:
the economy was in trouble because it was producing more
than people could afford to buy. "The cure," Roosevelt said
bluntly, "is not to produce so much."

So a strange struggle against production began. The daily stream of bills from the White House to the Capitol continued. First of the major New Deal measures was the Agricultural Adjustment Act. Owen D. Young, General Electric's chairman said, "If America burns her surplus wheat and cotton when men are hungry and unclothed elsewhere in the world, that fire will start a conflagration which we cannot stop." But under Agriculture Secretary Henry Wallace, the government paid farmers to plow crops under and kill little pigs. When large supplies of commodities persisted, the Commodity Credit Corporation (CCC) was set up to buy and store them.

At the time few people saw the New Deal as an underhanded power grab. "The whole country," one news story said, "has turned to government and implored it to take charge." Will Rogers remembered attending a Chamber of Commerce dinner with Jesse Jones, head of the Reconstruction Finance Corporation. As businessman after businessman took the podium to denounce big government, Jones would write on the back of his menu how much each had borrowed from the RFC.

The idea that businessmen were steadfast defenders of free markets against the overeducated Bolsheviks in the Roosevelt brains trust is fanciful. Businessmen were at least as frightened and puzzled as everyone else. The then-formidable National Association of Manufacturers officially approved a government scheme to check "demoralizing competition," coupled, "whimsically enough," *Business Week* said, with a resolution deploring "experiments in government." "The businessmen are the radicals," said Labor Secretary Frances Perkins. "Compared with them, I'm a conservative. They're willing to go to any length of government regulation if it will get them out of their trouble."

The result was the National Industrial Recovery Act (later NRA), the instrument through which businesses nationwide were enlisted in the crusade against production.

Under the NRA, business would limit production (it was called "adjusting supply to demand"), restrain competition so everyone would make a "reasonable" profit, abolish child labor, shorten the work week, and move wages up faster than prices. NRA's prototype had been designed by General Electric's Gerard Swope and known widely as the "Swope plan." Each segment of business was to write its own code—hundreds of them. The government would then make these codes mandatory. Business embraced this home-grown version of the corporate state enthusiastically. When NRA was passed, a quarter of a million New Yorkers marched in the streets to celebrate the end of the Great Depression.

"In war," the president said, "in the gloom of night attack, soldiers wear a bright badge on their shoulders to be sure that comrades do not fire on comrades. On that principle, those who cooperate in this program must know each other at a glance. That is why we have provided a badge of honor for this purpose, a simple design with a legend, 'We do our part,' and I ask that all those who join with me shall display that badge prominently. It is essential to our purpose."

The president picked General Hugh "Ironpants" Johnson to run NRA. A Lehman Brothers economist was his chief adviser. Johnson made the Blue Eagle NRA's emblem—"May Almighty God have mercy," he said, "on anyone who attempts to trifle with that bird."

The motion picture industry proposed a code that called for the virtual enslavement of actors—among other things, putting a $100,000 a year ceiling on their pay. When Eddie Cantor went to Warm Springs to protest, Roosevelt said, "I don't see why any actor should make more than I do." But in the end he withheld his approval of that code and killed it.

It all has the sound of musical comedy now, but then it was serious. The language was turned inside out. The "chiselers" were not merchants who raised prices but those who cut them. A Jersey City tailor went to prison for pressing a pair of pants for a nickel less than the code said he could. The public protested and Johnson let him off. But he had to promise to stay in line after that.

The Depression simply went on. Hawarden, Iowa, printed its own money to pay reliefers. Tenino, Washington, issued money made of wood, and twenty barter organizations in Seattle claimed 50,000 members. When the price of crude oil fell to ten cents a barrel, Oklahoma Governor "Alfalfa Bill" Murray called out the militia to stop oil production.

There was a surge of demand for draft animals. Al Capone started a soup kitchen in Chicago's Loop. More than one Midwestern county burned corn instead of coal because it was cheaper. When postage rates went from two cents to three, utilities began to deliver bills by hand. Great New York department stores were ordering sheets and towels a half dozen at a time. A writer asked a famous economist if there had been a comparable depression ever before. "Yes," he said, "it was called the Dark Ages and it lasted four hundred years."

The New Deal eventually ran into trouble with the Supreme Court. The Court upheld the money bills, but when it declared first NRA and then AAA unconstitutional, Roosevelt was outraged. He called the Justices the "nine old men" and tried to pack the Court, but members of both parties roared their disapproval and Roosevelt backed down. However, the Court did not turn back the New Deal. Except for NRA, the principal pieces survived in altered forms.

But when the economy failed to respond to the hopeful therapies of the New Deal, the tone of the public debate turned ugly. Roosevelt was never without opposition, but by 1936 there was a kind of cold panic in the air. "Some of these people," Roosevelt told a Chicago audience, "really forget how sick they were. I have their fever charts. I know how the knees of these rugged individualists were trembling four years ago and how their hearts fluttered. They came to Washington in great numbers. Washington did not look like a dangerous bureaucracy to them then. Oh no! It looked like an emergency hospital. All the distinguished patients wanted two things—a quick hypodermic to end the pain and a course of treatment to cure the disease. They wanted them in a hurry; we gave them

both. And now most of the patients seem to be doing very
nicely. Some of them are even well enough to throw their
crutches at the doctor." Huey Long, in a filibuster on the Senate floor, called the New Deal a "combination of the Stalin and
Hitler systems with a dash of Italian Fascism." When later
someone asked Long if Fascism would ever come to America,
he said, "Sure, but here it will be called anti-Fascism."

Father Charles Coughlin broadcast an evil brand of anti-
Semitic egalitarian populism to millions from his Charity Cru-
cifixion Tower in Royal Oak, Michigan. Upton Sinclair won
surprising support for his EPIC (End Poverty in California)
movement. Dr. Francis Everett Townsend, a retired doctor
from Long Beach, launched his "Townsend Plan" to give
everybody over sixty $200 a month for life. Technocracy, pro-
posing that energy units be substituted for money, was popular
for a while. Roosevelt's wily political adviser, Jim Farley, who
was not often wrong about politics, said if Huey Long hadn't
been assassinated on the steps of the Louisiana state house, he
would have beaten Roosevelt in 1936.

To run against Roosevelt in 1936, the Republicans nominated a bland Kansan named Alf Landon, who said that the
New Deal was a flop and campaigned on a platform to set enterprise free. Roosevelt termed this a belief that "that government is best which is most indifferent." Landon's emblem was
the sunflower. An appropriate choice, the president said: sun-
flowers are yellow, black-hearted, good only to feed parrots,
and always dead before November. Most of Roosevelt's business support dissolved; *Business Week* said that if Roosevelt
were re-elected he would seek to bring industry entirely under
the thumb of the federal government.

Postmaster General Farley predicted the president would
take all but two small New England states. When the election
proved him exactly right, Farley revised an old political
maxim. "As Maine goes," he said, "so goes Vermont."

At the end of 1936, Morgenthau said, in language Runyon
could have written, "Golly, I think we all got every reason to

face the new year with the greatest of complacence." But in August 1937, the economy collapsed in what is still the steepest decline in U.S. history.

The New Deal, contrary to the entrenched mythology, was a failure in its own terms. Unemployment stood at 9% in 1929. In the next four years, it moved in great surges to 25.1% (nearly 13 million) in 1933. Then, the rate declined slowly to 12.0% in 1937. But after the '37 slump, unemployment rebounded to 18.8% and stood at 16.7% when the Hitler-Stalin pact was signed on August 23, 1939.

The thirties seemed to be a decade cursed by destiny. As if history's worst depression were not enough, drought and wind drove thousands of desperate farmers from the Dust Bowl. In 1937, the Ohio River flooded and left 700,000 homeless. A year later the worst hurricane within memory devastated the New England coast.

The Crash of '37 was to be the beginning of the end of the New Deal. In December 1943, after a candid interview with Roosevelt, *Time* magazine reported that the New Deal, after a lingering illness, was dead. Thus began the era of John Maynard Keynes, one in which the idea of independent action on the public business would recede still further. Before Keynes, it appeared only that the independent sector had tried and failed to cope with the problem of mass unemployment. After Keynes, it appeared that it never could—that the sector would always, in the nature of things, be useless against unemployment.

The economic consequences of Keynes have been exhaustively chronicled, but much less has been said about the unexpected social consequences of his thought, which in the long run may prove to have greater impact and be less readily reversible. For Keynesian economic policy, or, more accurately, the social overtones of his economic policy, profoundly altered the institutional balance of American society.

5

The Mind of Maynard Keynes

"We are all Keynesians now."
Richard Milhous Nixon
"I am not a Keynesian."
John Maynard Keynes

In 1936, the year of Roosevelt's landslide re-election, *The General Theory of Employment, Interest and Money* was published in England and a "new" economics was born to a waiting world. A group of impatient Harvard students pooled their money and ordered copies direct from the English publisher. One economist described his rapture on first reading *The General Theory* by quoting Wordsworth's lines on the French Revolution: "Bliss was it in that dawn to be alive, but to be young was very heaven."

Its author, John Maynard Keynes is, next to Virginia Woolf, the best remembered member of the inner circle of Bloomsbury—England's gifted, energetic, abrasive, snobbish, neurotic, and immensely influential group of "loving friends."

His father, John Neville Keynes, an economist and logician, was a Cambridge don of great distinction, as well as the University's registrar. His mother was once mayor of Cambridge.

As a boy Keynes did his homework in his father's study and read the proofs of his father's books. By the end of his years at Eton, according to Bloomsbury's best chronicler, Leon Edel, "he lived in the school as if it were his own fine country house and (in a lavender waistcoat) cooperated with his friends in running it."

At Cambridge, a visitor described him as a person whom no

one could overlook, everyone respected, and some liked. Desmond McCarthy said Keynes' object in life then seemed to be to impress men of forty. A hobby, one of many, was climbing mountains.

Keynes was, from the first, an ugly, irresistible man. He was a tall, awkward figure at Cambridge, with thick lips and bad teeth, but his smile was electrifying.

He encountered the core of his lifelong Bloomsbury intimates as a member of the Apostles, a secret society of Cambridge's intellectual upper crust that dated from Tennyson's time. The society had included Alfred North Whitehead, Bertrand Russell, and E. M. Forster. Keynes found the Apostles' adored philosopher, G. E. Moore's, *Principia Ethica* "entrancing" and envied the "timeless ecstasy" in which Moore seemed to live. "We accepted Moore's religion," Keynes wrote later, "and discarded his morals."

Above all, Apostles believed themselves to be "different from ordinary people," distinguished by exceptional energy, intellect, and sensibility. But D. H. Lawrence was appalled by what he called their "brittleness," and the philosopher Wittgenstein, finding the group emotionally juvenile, resigned soon after he was elected.

Bertrand Russell praised Keynes' intellect as "the sharpest and cleverest I have ever known," but wondered whether his cleverness was "incompatible with depth." Russell believed his opponents were villains; Keynes thought his merely idiots. Bloomsbury chronicler Michael Holroyd acknowledged the "extraordinary speed of his brain" but found "some imaginative quality" strangely lacking. "The brilliant sparkle of his writing," Holroyd said, "is not superficial, but rather icy. Like a barrister, he was often bent on putting over a point of view at one remove from himself, and his stated opinions seemed on occasion to be oddly vicarious. . . . With all his great charm [Keynes'] view of things remained cold and almost mechanical."

And much later Keynes himself wrote of those early days, "I

can see us as water spiders, gracefully skimming, as light and reasonable as air, the surface of the stream without any contact at all with the eddies and currents beneath."

Edel describes Keynes at Cambridge as a reformer disguised as a rebel, who loved the Establishment which sustained him while he railed against it and mocked its morals.

At Cambridge, Keynes wrote, in one of the century's looming understatements, "I find economics increasingly satisfactory and I think I am rather good at it."

After Cambridge, Keynes served some time as an India office civil servant, found it a bore and after a few years returned to Cambridge. When World War I erupted, he hurried from Cambridge to Whitehall on a borrowed motorcycle to prevent, if he could, a panic-induced increase in the bank rate. He worked for the Treasury throughout the war and was a prominent figure at the Versailles peace negotiations. A colleague said that "in front of a large map he has the range of an eagle."

Keynes was famous for his occasionally withering rudeness, but he charmed most people he met. Lady Ottoline Morrell, the reigning lioness of London society, suspected that Keynes wanted from life only a succession of agreeable moments and was troubled by his bisexuality, but nevertheless responded to his "detached, meditating and yet half caressing interest in those he is speaking to, head on one side, a kindly tolerant smile and very charming eyes wandering, searching, speculating."

He watched the world about him intently and was passionately curious about people's hands (FDR's he found "firm and fairly strong" but "not clever or with finesse"). His own hands he often tucked away, each in the sleeve of the other, like a mandarin.

Keynes' first attempt to fashion a "new economics," his *Treatise on Money*, published in 1930, was flawed and failed to ignite. But the publication of *The General Theory*, in 1936, led to the instant apotheosis of Keynes and Keynesianism—an event that will no doubt be remembered as one of the wonders of intellectual history. America's Great Depression was then in its seventh year.

Keynes' conquest of the academic mind depended first of all on his ability to demonstrate that the unemployment that persisted cruelly through the thirties (or seemed to)* was not induced by mistaken monetary policy but stemmed from a deep systemic flaw. It was a question of replacing the proposition that a free economy was essentially self-stabilizing with its opposite: that a maturing industrial economy *tended* to come to rest without its resources fully employed. Investment opportunities tended to fall behind the rate of saving, but the old patterns of saving persisted anyway. Unemployment was not an ephemeral phenomenon that would sooner or later correct itself: it was endemic to a free economy.

The Keynesian vision expressed in *The General Theory* was a vision of stagnation—a world with vanishing frontiers and dwindling opportunities, one in which the need for capital was declining and in which the social function of saving had disappeared—a world in which, in fact, saving made things worse.

The idea of planned deficits to get a stalled economy moving was familiar. But Keynes added in *The General Theory* the revolutionary proposition that monetary management was not a temporary expedient, but should become the basis for a general and continuing form of economic therapy.

A senile economy would forever tend to doze off on its own and would have to be shocked into wakefulness again and again by some outside force—namely government deficits. The economy would not function without continuous intervention, guided by the economics we now know as "macro" economics. The era of monetary engineering had arrived. Overnight, economics became an activist, interventionist discipline. It was as if physicists had discovered that the earth would no longer turn by itself and would henceforth have to be kept moving by

---

* Economist Michael Darby, contends that unemployment was grossly overestimated because from 2 to 3½ million public employees were inadvertently not counted as employed.

some contrived outside force. The idea of scientific detachment seemed dangerously out of date.

Keynesian economics was not so much accepted as swallowed. It quickly became less a school of thought than a new economic church, completely furnished, as journalist Garet Garrett wrote later, with "all the properties proper to a church, such as a revelation of its own, a rigid doctrine, a symbolic language, a propaganda, a priestcraft and a demonology." And Harvard's Joseph Schumpeter saw clearly that economic teachings alone could never arouse such ardent constituencies "unless the cold steel of analysis derives a temperature not naturally its own" from the theory's political overtones.

Keynes provided what the world was waiting for: an elaborate rationalization of the festering antagonism to capitalism. Only the belief in the apparent absolute need for saving had caused people to tolerate capitalism's infuriating inequalities. Classical economics had taught that progress—in which all would share, however unequally—depended on saving and that the rich, who saved most, were most necessary to progress. Keynes stood that proposition on its head. Saving was not only not necessary; it was the principal cause of unemployment. Thus the unequal distribution of income, the circumstance people most resented, was the cause of unemployment, the problem they most feared.

Two centuries of pent-up anticapitalist feeling could now be let loose in the public interest. The Spanish philosopher-statesman Ortega y Gasset had said, "When people want bread, they begin by destroying the bakeries." Keynes transformed this impulse into the semblance of sound public policy. He appealed to the radicals among us—and to the radical streak in most of us—when he wrote, "the growth of wealth, so far from being dependent on the abstinence of the rich, as is commonly supposed, is more likely to be impeded by it." Keynes' vision was an alluring one of capitalism without capitalists, a utopia to be attained peacefully through economic policy without a tiresome revolution. In the "Concluding Notes" to *The General Theory* he wrote: "I see, therefore, the rentier [investor] aspect of capitalism as a transitional phase which will disappear when it has done its work. And with the disappearance of its rentier aspect much else in it besides will suffer a sea change. It will be, moreover, a great advantage . . . that the euthanasia of the rentier, of the functionless investor, will be nothing sudden, merely a gradual but prolonged continuance of what we have seen recently in Great Britain, and will need no revolution."

Thus the ambivalence Edel discerned in the young Apostle Keynes was reconciled. At Cambridge he was a reformer disguised as a rebel. In the end, he fomented rebellion through reform.

Until the slump of 1937 Roosevelt was not a Keynesian. In 1896, as a schoolboy at Groton, he'd written in his notebook: "A glut of capital is impossible until everyone has everything he wishes, but there may be too much capital invested in a particular business; in that case capital will be withdrawn and will seek investment elsewhere." And this proposition of classical economics was Keynes' primary target.

But there was other, perhaps more basic, common ground. At Harvard, Roosevelt had heard the frontier thesis from its very source—from Frederick Jackson Turner himself. America had been shaped by its frontiers, Turner said, and if the day came when the frontiers were gone and our national restlessness had no physical outlet, it might be turned outward in imperialist adventuring or inward in the form of demands that the government appease working class discontent.

The idea that there is a limit to growth had for years been a favorite Roosevelt theme. A few weeks before his election in 1932, he had told an audience of San Francisco businessmen that America's great era of growth was over. (Roosevelt aide and brainstruster Adolph Berle wrote the speech on short notice in an effort to raise the intellectual level of the campaign.)

"Our industrial plant is built," Roosevelt said. "Our last frontier has long since been reached, and there is practically no
more free land. More than half of our people no longer live on
farms . . . and cannot derive a living by cultivating their own
property. There is no safety valve in the form of a Western
prairie to which those thrown out of work by the Eastern economic machines can go for a new start. . . ." Our task now, he
concluded, "is *not* discovery of exploitation of natural resources or producing more goods. It is the soberer, less dramatic business of administering resources and plants already at
hand."

A few weeks later, in Madison Square Garden, Herbert
Hoover reproached FDR for sounding again the "same note of
pessimism in economic depressions going back for one hundred years. What Governor Roosevelt has overlooked is that
we are yet but on the frontiers of development of science and
of invention."

Tugwell, the only economist in the Roosevelt brains trust,
blamed the recession on Frederick Winslow Taylor, the father
of time-study, the apostle of scientific management, whom
Tugwell accused of having made production excessively efficient. "If," Tugwell wrote, "we had had eyes to see the impli-
cations of Taylor's work, we should have known that the vast
expansion of production which must follow would clog all the
old channels of trade, swamp the mechanisms of an artificially
limited commerce and end in a period of violent reconstruction."

And here at least, in a dismal view of the future of an un-
managed economy, the Keynesians, the New Dealers, and the
frightened population converged. As the Great Depression
wore on, people began to suspect it was not just a temporary
spasm of instability resulting from a passing imbalance of demand and supply: the United States economy was coming to
the end of the road—what are now called the limits of growth
had been reached. The economy was not sick; it was senile. It
would never again produce enough buying power to maintain

its momentum or enough jobs to keep everyone employed. And an entire generation of workers who had lately left the land and become wholly dependent on their wages were terror-stricken. Millions believed they might never have a job again.

More and more Americans began to believe that the moment working people had dreaded since the earliest beginnings of industrialization had arrived at last. The world's work was done. Instead of stretching the work out, the way we sensed we should have—making it last—we had done it all too quickly. The Luddites were right. The machine was the enemy of the working man. It had lured him away from the land and then, when the work was completed, left him to starve.

Before the Civil War, an American periodical predicted solemnly that machines would soon do all the work and bring on universal unemployment. And eighty years ago, in Buffalo, a crowd of day laborers and their wives wrecked a street-paving machine.

Soon after Roosevelt's election, Keynes told him in an open letter to *The New York Times* plainly what needed to be done: "I lay overwhelming emphasis on the increase of national purchasing power resulting from government expenditure which is financed by loans and is not merely a transfer through taxation from existing incomes."*

But Roosevelt did not at first seem to like the Keynesian medicine. Felix Frankfurter arranged for the economist to visit the president in 1934, a visit of which Roosevelt wrote, "I had a grand talk with K and liked him immensely. . . ." But he complained to Frances Perkins that Keynes had left behind "a whole rigamarole of figures. He must be more of a mathematician than a political economist." And Keynes said coolly he had "supposed the president was more literate, economically speaking."

---

* In 1931 Keynes believed that spending for recovery was at best a limited cure, a kind of "tonic to change business conditions." "There is nothing," he said, "President Hoover can do that an earthquake could not do better."

In any case, Keynes had failed so far to seduce Roosevelt, who balked at his central prescription. Roosevelt was perfectly willing to tolerate deficits if the public works he initiated to provide employment could not be paid for by taxes. But Keynes' belief (shared by many if not most economists at the time) that the deficit itself was the cure for unemployment was an idea Roosevelt could not yet digest.

When, after the Crash of '37, Keynes again urged more courageous spending on FDR in another open letter in early 1938, the advice was again rejected. But soon after, with the economy still declining, the Keynesian members of the brains trust finally prevailed. Beardsley Ruml, a Macy's department store executive, proposed deliberate deficit spending and somehow Harry Hopkins sold the idea to Roosevelt. We needed, Ruml reasoned, an $88 billion national income for full employment. But national income was only $56 billion. Assuming money turns over 2 or 3 times a year, the economy would need another $7 to $10 billion. Perhaps as much as $4 billion would come from private investment, leaving a "deficit" of $3 to $6 billion. For government to provide $6 billion was out of the question, but $3 billion might be possible. This became the basis of the recovery plan Roosevelt presented to the nation in a fireside chat in April. Thus, Roosevelt discovered retrospectively that he was a Keynesian.

Even then, according to Morgenthau, Roosevelt was not really reconciled to deficit spending. He accepted the propositions of Keynes not because he believed in them but because they were a tailor-made rationalization of an unexpected and unwelcome reality. *The General Theory* was just what the New Dealers needed—an explanation for the economy's continued malaise that exonerated the New Deal. The economy's sickness was the result of mature capitalism's deadly propensity for private investment to lag full-employment saving.

Herbert Stein writes, in *The Fiscal Revolution in America*, probably the best history of the period, "In 1939 the country was unwilling to commit itself to spending as a way to prosperity . . . the government would spend as an emergency measure

. . . to get out of 'the bottom of the well' . . . but it was not prepared to regularize and perpetuate the process." The public
still believed three to one in balanced budgets.

On September 1, 1939, Hitler marched into Poland, and two
days later England and France declared war on Germany:
World War II had begun. Simultaneously, the American economy was found to have vast resources of idle manpower,
money, and ingenuity waiting to be put to use.

In December 1940, 1,239,000 Americans were on welfare.
In the next thirty months that figure fell 72%—to 347,000. Unemployment fell from almost 17% to 1.2%. A study of Seneca,
Illinois, showed the same pattern in microcosm. In 1942,
twenty Seneca families were receiving county assistance. In
1943, the figure fell to four. By 1944, there was only one. That
Christmas the Women's Christian Temperance Union couldn't
find a single family in all of Illinois that needed a Christmas
basket. (Still, rates of delinquency increased, and the conventional wisdom that links poverty and delinquency was briefly
called into question.) "What are we liberals after?" a *Common
Sense* writer wanted to know. "The honest-minded liberal will
admit that the common man is getting a better break than ever
he did under the New Deal."

During the war, I worked on the swing shift of a little oil re-
finery in West Los Angeles. All of us—myself a teenager, a
man in his late sixties, an alcoholic, an illegal immigrant, a
woman with a prison record, a homosexual—would have been
thought unemployable a few months before.

The wartime achievements of the American economy, so
recently pronounced senile, were astonishing. Two things
were striking about the U.S. production effort: the lightning
speed of the transition by an economy that had been in slow
motion for a decade and the heights of productivity attained
by an economy that had presumably reached the limits of
growth.

In 1939, the United States ranked nineteenth as a world military power. In 1940, our army was still smaller than Holland's.
We had emptied our arsenals to rearm the British Army,

which had left its weapons on the beaches of Dunkirk. U.S. draftees were training with wooden rifles. We had no large-scale munitions industry, and only about 500 tanks and 5000 military planes. Half of the army's 2 million rifles were 1903 Springfields. In less than a year, American industry retooled and was outproducing Germany, Italy, and Japan put together. Factories half idle months before began to work around the clock.

What on Pearl Harbor Day had been a cornfield in Michigan, in one year was the site of a factory producing a four-engined bomber every hour. In less than a year, Detroit was making tanks as fast as it had been turning out cars. A construction company with no shipbuilding experience before Pearl Harbor was turning out merchant ships faster than the German U-boats could sink them. For the first time in history we were making lathes on the assembly line. A merry-go-round manufacturer was making gun mounts. A mattress factory converted to machine gun belts. A builder of burial vaults found himself turning out bombs. A refrigerator company was making airplane wings; railroad car makers converted to tanks; and a textile mill produced antitank-gun carriages.

Roosevelt's production chiefs were flabbergasted when he stated his goals. For example, he called for 20,000 planes when in twenty years the industry had produced only 30,000. But, during the war, with Detroit's help, it built 300,000.

In 1939, there were 50,000 people building airplanes. Four years later, there were 2 million. Lockheed's sales increased from $35 million in 1939 to $668 million in 1943.

Charles Sorensen of Ford went to Washington with a twenty-foot-long blueprint of a plant he claimed could produce a bomber an hour. The government began to build Willow Run in April 1941, and eleven months later B-24s were coming off the line. *Business Week* called the conversion of the automobile industry "the biggest cutting-up job in industry history, a job of deliberate destruction on a multi-billion dollar scale that defies the imagination."

Henry J. Kaiser, a grade-school dropout who had already worked miracles in big construction, built 1500 Liberty Ships—about one a day—throughout the war, a pace the world had not seen since the days of the Venetian *Arsenale*. Our merchant fleet quintupled.

The railroads had already begun to show signs of infirmity, but in five years passenger volume increased 4½ times and freight traffic 2½ times.

At first there were sudden disabling shortages of raw materials: aluminum, magnesium, rubber, and many others. Half the U.S. rubber supply was cut off when war broke out. We produced a pitiful 1000 tons of synthetic rubber in 1939. Five years later, in 1944, we produced 836,000 tons. The production of consumer goods rose 25% between 1939 and 1941.

On D-Day, June 6, 1944, the Normandy invasion, called "Overlord," history's largest military operation, was launched. It involved 4000 ships, 11,000 planes, and countless landing craft. A storm beached 300 ships and destroyed most of the artificial harbors we had sunk in the shallows, but by then the supply stream was so strong it was only a minor setback. Eisenhower, the supreme commander, said later, "No sight so impressed me with the industrial might of America as the wreckage on the landing beaches. For any other nation the disaster would have been decisive; but so great was America's productive capacity that the great storm occasioned no more than a ripple in our military build-up."

Stalin, whose Red Army had lost half a million men at Stalingrad, put it plainly in a toast at Teheran. "To American production," he said, "without which this war would have been lost."

The New Deal had not confirmed the soundness of the Keynesian theory, but the experience of the war seemed to do so perfectly. The Keynesians had contended, when spending had not seemed to lift the economy, that the scale had been far too timid, that some really courageous spending was what was wanted. What the New Deal had done reluctantly was right in principle, but not nearly enough.

Federal spending jumped from $9 billion in 1940 to more than $100 billion in 1945. In 1941, the deficit was $5 billion; by 1943 it was over $45 billion. Government's wartime deficits totaled nearly $200 billion. The national perspective had been radically altered. The government had invested billions directly in plants and equipment. And much of what was produced was destroyed.

Keynes had used Egypt's pyramids to illustrate how spending need have no utility to have value as an economic stimulant. (As if born to the role of prophet, Keynes could be profound, eloquent, cryptic, contradictory, and maddening. A critic who found the idea of artificially creating purposeless work absurd asked Lord Keynes if raising white elephants would be a reasonable example of what he meant. "Yes," Keynes replied, "that would be just the thing.") The production of weapons is the ultimate example: output was not simply consumed; it was demolished.

The carrier *Hornet*, for example, cost $60 million; when it was sunk, $60 million had been created and spent to no surviving purpose. The money spent for the *Hornet*, along with other billions of wartime spending, turned loose in an economy that had been foundering for a decade, had apparently done what neither independent action nor even New Deal government action could do: it had brought the economy to life, eliminated unemployment, and conquered poverty. That was the real beginning of the age of Keynes.

A Keynesian wrote later, "The huge federal deficits generated by massive military expenditure produced precisely the consequences anticipated by the Keynesians. What counted was the spending. A society sensible enough to purchase decent health care, public transportation, public libraries, and inexpensive shelter, could also enjoy the delights of full employment."

6

The Forgotten Revolution

"The people, using their government as an agent, found the means to lick the depression. Now we are employing the same means of well-designed government programs to help strengthen and steadily expand the national economy."

Harry S Truman

All through the war, Keynesian concepts continued to work their way into the thinking of policymakers.

In March 1943, the tide of battle had barely begun to turn. Rommel was just starting to lose ground in North Africa, and the Allies had yet to regain an inch of territory in the Pacific. But the National Resources Planning Board issued a lyrical vision of the America that was to be after the war: "The upsurging human personality, even in the terrible grip of war, looks for new heavens and the new earth within its sight and grasp for the first time." The report laid out "A New Bill of Rights," the first of which was "the right to work usefully and creatively through the productive years" and including, at the end, "the right to rest, recreation and adventure, the opportunity to enjoy life and to take part in an advancing civilization." You could buy a copy for a dime. Congress read the report and strangled the agency.

But two years later, in his State of the Union Message, the president himself called for a "second" bill of rights, and said, "Of these rights, the most fundamental, and one on which the fulfillment of the others in large degree depends, is the right to a useful and remunerative job."

As early as 1944, "full employment" had been almost universally accepted as the central ambition of the modern state. Pollster Elmo Roper asked, in the fall of 1944, "If at any time there are not sufficient jobs in private employment to go around, then government can and must create additional job opportunities because there must be jobs for all in this country of ours." Of the people polled, 68% agreed, about the same percentage as believed in balanced budgets.

Full employment as the principal domestic policy goal almost instantly became bipartisan. Republican presidential candidate Thomas E. Dewey campaigned for it in 1944.

It was irresistible, supported not only by the positive vision of a world of joy and fulfillment but also by the awful specter of a postwar depression worse than the thirties.

It seemed likely that a mature economy, presumably prone to a loss of momentum without monetary stimulation, would collapse, and it was widely predicted that it would.

Two days before the Pacific War ended, a Washington newspaperman warned that 10 million workers would be out of work in a month. A few days later the War Production Board predicted 7 to 9 million unemployed by Thanksgiving. *The New York Times* said that the "best" government and private sources predicted 8 million unemployed by spring 1946. Even *The Wall Street Journal* saw 6.2 million unemployed by the end of the year. The national nightmare was of returning veterans still in uniform selling apples in the street as some of their fathers had done.

And by now the therapy seemed obvious. Vice President Henry Wallace proposed permanent peacetime government spending at wartime levels to keep employment "full."

After World War I, the dollar-a-year men who had run the business side of the war from Washington put on their hats and went home. Woodrow Wilson gave a pep talk to American business, and that was the extent of economic demobilization. This time it would be different.

The health of the U.S. economy would henceforth be the government's business. The weapon would be spending. Spending would come first. That was understood. In the past, the purpose of federal spending had been the first consideration. Now, the level of spending would be decided and only then its objects. But, Macy's executive Beardsley Ruml assured the public in a 1943 radio talk, the policy didn't mean "spending for its own sake." There would never need to be "wasteful spending." (Here, of course, he parted momentarily from Keynes, who sometimes seemed to say that wasteful spending was best.) "When government lends or spends, it should put its money into projects that are really necessary, efficient and productive." And who could doubt that in our unfinished society there could ever be a lack of "really necessary" projects?

The Keynesians began to diverge from Keynes. While Keynes' American disciples were predicting a major postwar recession and urging large spending programs, Keynes was writing to an American correspondent that inflation rather than unemployment would be the problem in America "for some time to come."

By the end of the war, talk of balancing the budget had become, according to economist Herbert Stein, "pure ritual."

Henry Wallace spelled it all out in recognizably Keynesian language: "The essential idea is that the federal government is ultimately responsible for full employment and can discharge its responsibility by planning in advance to synchronize all of its programs with the programs of private enterprise so that the whole national income will be maintained at the full employment level."

The president said: "It is the responsibility of the government to insure sustained markets. Then and only then can free enterprise provide jobs."

The commitment would be, above all, open-ended. In what was called the Employment Act of 1946, or the National Job Budget Bill, it became "the responsibility of the federal government to provide such volume of federal investment and expenditure as may be needed to assure continuing full employment." The Act called on government to use "all its plans, functions and resources" to accomplish its purpose.

The details would, of course, be immensely complicated,

but the essentials of the system imagined by the bill were straightforward. The government would figure out how much spending of all kinds would be required to maintain employment at some desired level—such as 60 million jobs. Then government economists would estimate how much all the non-federal entities—families, businesses, state and local governments, and so forth—were likely to spend. The difference between the level of spending needed to produce full employment and estimated nonfederal spending would be made up by federal spending—preferably for necessary programs but certainly for something.

The conservative minds among us were aghast. The Act seemed to repeal the Protestant ethic, free enterprise, and sanity all at once.

The National Resources Planning Board said, "One of the important economic facts we have learned in the past decades is that fiscal and monetary policy can be and should be used to foster an expanding economy. We need not be afraid. . . ."

It all bypassed the tiresome argument about the comparative advantages of capitalism and socialism. It was, as Sir William Beveridge wrote in his vastly influential *Full Employment in a Free Society*, a matter of socializing demand rather than production. In England, they soon did both.

When President Harry S Truman signed the Employment Act on February 20, 1946, he called it "a commitment to take any and all of the measures necessary for a healthy economy." It was a new day. Two months later, Keynes died at Tilton.

The commitment expressed in the Employment Act launched what was to become the most extensive and expensive government project in the history of the world, including the pyramids and the Great Wall of China. It was a blank check to pay whatever it cost to achieve something which, in the first place, could never be more than approximately defined and which, in the second place, might or might not respond to the techniques the federal government might invent. Above all, it was a commitment that was incompatible with the idea of fiscal restraint.

The serious hazards in a politically administered full employment policy were clear to some from the beginning. Keynes had many gifted critics, like the Austrian economist F. A. Hayek, who warned that artificial demand stimulation would not cause real recovery, only the appearance of it. Deficit spending would in time produce progressive inflation, as ever-larger deficits were required to sustain the illusion of prosperity. And in the long run, stimulating demand artificially would create more unemployment than it set out to prevent. Keynes himself was uneasy. A few months before his death he complained to a friend, an American economist, that "the easy money policy is being pushed too far." His friend suggested he write another book.

Had there been no war, the failure of the New Deal might have produced a careful and illuminating dissection of the experience of the thirties. But the war and its apparent validation of Keynesian theory eliminated that possibility, and the combination of conjecture and rationalization on which New Deal policies were built became the new basis of public policy.

Mr. Roosevelt began by saying, "It is the first time in our history that the nation as a whole and regardless of party has approved drastic changes in the methods and forms of the functions of government, without destroying the basic principles." Later he put it more frankly: "If it was a revolution, it was a peaceful one."

The revolutionary aspects of the period were several. In the first place, there was a revolution in the national attitude toward public outlays. Economy in government had once been a cardinal virtue, for the public was aware that easy carelessness with money was typical of monopolies in general and of governments in particular and was wary of that tendency. Now it was different. Government spending became its own justification, thought to have value as an economic stimulant, aside from the merits of the programs it financed. (This is the origin of the liberal's legendary unconcern about the cost of government programs, which so infuriates conservatives.) Here was a politician's dream: spending was presumed to be a good thing, and the burden of proving the contrary was subtly shifted to its opponents. Profligacy in the service of stability was not a vice. Congress no longer needed to choose among programs: it could enact them all.

Related to this was another revolutionary proposition: programs that transfer income from savers to spenders have utility beyond their benefits to individuals—they tend to keep the economy moving. Americans had never been very receptive to the perennial proposals to redistribute wealth politically, and giving voters direct access to the Treasury had been considered imprudent and politically perilous. Now the idea of taking from the saving rich and giving to the spending poor was clothed in the public interest, and the historical reluctance of Americans to use the power of government to redistribute our wealth was overcome.

Another revolutionary proposition was that production is not a major consideration and can safely be ignored. It tends to follow automatically if demand is kept strong. No longer were little pigs destroyed, or cornfields set on fire, or troops sent to stop oil production. The passionate antagonism to production that had characterized the thirties had cooled. But an official indifference to the need to maintain and expand productive capacity became a permanent part of public policy.

Another proposition was more general. Before the New Deal, the principal federal presence in most American communities had been the Post Office. But by the end of the war, a staggering number of offices and bureaus had been established. The government had built a broad base from which to grow.

Theodore Roosevelt opened his own mail and answered much of it in longhand. Woodrow Wilson typed his own speeches. Hoover's White House staff was forty-two. Roosevelt's was 597. Truman's was 1178. Congress, perhaps suspecting the government was already expanding uncontrollably, set up a commission to study the question and asked Hoover to head it. The first Hoover Commission reported in effect that government had even then, in the late forties, become so large as to be almost incomprehensible. The commission produced a shelf of books; the summary alone was 500 closely printed pages.

After the New Deal, the government was licensed to police the behavior of business on a broad front. In addition, the public had begun to treat business as a separate and sinister force in society, and business has since had to struggle against a strong undertow of doubt about its legitimacy. The public's impulses to punish business and to reform it were hopelessly mixed together.

To no one's surprise, the "temporary" abandonment of the gold standard in the early days of the New Deal became permanent, and government could meet deficits quite painlessly, if not by borrowing, then simply by issuing promises to pay that were legally defined as money. The kind of money colonial Americans had contemptuously called "shinplasters" had become the only money we had.

Deficits themselves took on a new legitimacy. What had been an embarrassed last resort to be used only in time of war or catastrophe became the accepted medicine against the system's most dreaded disability.

And if the state could solve the curse of unemployment, could it then not do almost anything it put its mind to? Americans began to think of the federal government as omnicompetent. So began an era of fervent confidence—almost religious in its intensity—in the social utility of centralization.

Even the opponents of centralization rarely challenged the competence of the state. Conservatives were worried about power—whether a government with large responsibilities would need great power that might someday be difficult to control. Businessmen opposed high taxes (then as now, they opposed taxes much more fiercely than spending). Dissenting economists harped on the inflationary hazards of a full-employment policy. But the *effectiveness* of centralization has only lately been called into question. Critics could say that big government was dangerous; the rich could complain that the taxes they paid to support it were inconvenient; but hardly anyone doubted it would work.

Along with the economic changes was another less widely advertised aspect of the revolution. By 1946, after years of depression and war, the American tradition of independent action on the public business had been buried alive. This may prove to have been the most serious casualty of the Keynesian revolution.

The belief that government spending was the ultimate weapon against unemployment gave government an overwhelming advantage in the continuing contention for social responsibility. Overnight, in good times and in bad, almost every proposal for expanding the role of government had a powerful, seemingly conclusive new justification. By freeing government from the discipline of cost consciousness, the balance between the public and independent sectors was radically—perhaps permanently—tilted in favor of centralization.

The decline of the independent sector was never debated; it had no inherent capacity for self-defense. America's most distinctive social tradition was consigned to the shadows with hardly a murmur of protest.

Tocqueville had written in what has become the most quoted tribute to the early vigor of "the immense assemblage of organizations" in America's independent sector: "The Americans make associations to give entertainments, to found seminaries, to build inns, to construct churches, to diffuse books, to send missionaries to the antipodes; in this manner they found hospitals, prisons and schools. . . . Whenever at the head of some new undertaking you see the government in France, or a man of rank in England, in the United States you will be sure to find an association. . . . Nothing . . . is more deserving of our attention. . . ."

But in 1944, Swedish economist Gunnar Myrdal wrote in *An American Dilemma:* "They [the American masses] are accustomed to being static and receptive. . . . They do not know how to cooperate and how to pool risks for a common goal. They do not meet much. They do not organize. They do not speak for themselves."

And almost twenty years later, in *Challenge to Affluence*, he wrote: "The citizen's participation in public life, taken in its broadest terms, is lower in America than generally in countries that are similar to it in basic values."

The idea that Americans would band together to *do* something—to build an opera house or find jobs for people who were somehow handicapped or set safety standards for electric toasters—was displaced by another. Americans began to form committees to implore the government to act. And the state, which tends to expand even without encouragement, grew rapidly. The essential distinction between society and the state began to blur. In 1981, in Burlington, Vermont, the socialist mayor kicked off the local United Fund campaign by suggesting that private philanthropy be eliminated.

Liberals and conservatives agree that the independent sector is no longer capable of dealing with the problems of the industrial age. George Gilder, whose book *Wealth and Poverty* became the Bible of the Reagan administration, observed that as American society has become mobile, individualistic, and atomized, "the old modes of private assistance . . . no longer suffice." And, at the other end of the ideological spectrum, economist Robert Heilbroner agrees that "individuals . . . could not cope unaided in a society that was no longer personal and small-town, but impersonal, big-city."

A Columbia economist considered the independent sector fit only for tasks such as maintaining dog cemeteries or bird sanctuaries or the climbing of Mount Everest. But, he added, "airtight examples of this sort are increasingly hard to find." Beatrice and Sidney Webb, Britain's socialist pioneers, saw voluntary organizations merely as an "extension ladder" that would add a little to the reach of the state.

Thus, after a decade and a half of depression and war, the role of the independent sector had practically disappeared; it had been pushed off, out of sight, into small, unimportant reservations of responsibility. Harvard's John Kenneth Galbraith could write: "... functions accrue to the state because, as a purely technical matter, there is no alternative to public management."

Americans would continue to sing the praises of pluralism, but the nation had become a society with two important sectors and the vestige of a third.

In 1958 Galbraith's best-selling *The Affluent Society* discussed the division of responsibility between two sectors—the "public" by which he meant government, and the "private," by which he meant business. He made no mention of a third sector. As far as I know, no one noticed the omission for years.

There was thus no limit to the potential size or scope of government, and the public business could no longer be accurately defined. There would be no way to measure the effectiveness of government programs. The idea of limited government had given way to the idea of a welfare state, which would in time give way to the idea of the full-service state. There would be a tendency for the size of government to increase even as its effectiveness decreased; a tendency for the beneficiaries and benefits of government programs to increase geometrically; a tendency for the governmental sector's claims on the private sector to increase until it undermined the latter's capacity to produce; a tendency for government first to push its taxing powers to the limit, then to borrow to the limit and finally to finance its expansion by habitual inflation.

The result of the rejection of the third, independent sector has been the creation of a society that is, as Lord Bryce said in another connection, all sail and no anchor. To no one's surprise, reversing a century-old pattern, the federal government has grown much, much faster than the rest of the society.

7

The Looking Glass War on Unemployment

". . . his education had had the curious effect of making things
that he read and wrote more real to him than things he saw.
Statistics about agricultural labourers were the substance; any
real ditcher, ploughman or farmer's boy, was the shadow . . . in
his own way, he believed as firmly as any mystic in the superior
reality of things that are not seen."

C. S. Lewis
That Hideous Strength

In his novel *The Looking Glass War,* John Le Carré describes a
doomed undertaking, an act of espionage, executed in the sixties using the methods of the forties. A foolproof plan, elabo-
rately conceived and refined, and rehearsed in a hypothetical
world, was carried out in a real one. It was a catastrophe. An
agent was selected and carefully trained by obsolete methods
in the use of obsolete equipment. When he finally made his
"run," the agent was under surveillance from the moment he
entered enemy territory, his observers puzzled only by his un-
believable clumsiness.

Similarly, over the years, the "war" on unemployment became more and more detached from reality, and the effort to
stabilize the economy an isolated exercise. Originally, the
numbers used to guide these activities were meant to represent, at least approximately, something real. The unemployment figure quickly became the primary gauge of the health of
the economy. Was or was not the economy providing enough

jobs? The public's central concern was embodied in this sacred statistic, and it has been assumed that except for the statistical errors that soften extrapolations from samples, the rate described a reality.

The unemployment figure is usually reported to the first decimal place, which seems to imply precision. It is supposed to mean first of all the percent of the labor force that cannot find work. But we must be forgiven if we expect it to bear some relationship to the situation in the thirties, when the number first began to be compiled.

During the first full year of the Great Depression, for example, unemployment reached 7.8%, meaning that almost 4 million workers were unemployed. That was a desperate time, and those 4 million—or most of them—were in serious distress.

But today's unemployment figure is useless as an indicator of human emergency. In 1977 (any recent year will serve the purpose) the number reached 7.0%, meaning about 7½ million people were "unemployed." Seven million were receiving unemployment insurance. At that time, 15 million Americans were on welfare and 19 million were receiving food stamps. The Bureau of Labor Statistics has reported that nearly a third of the unemployed have turned down at least one job offer. Everyone knows people who are *seeking* unemployment, who are employed at being unemployed. Thousands of them are asking that their unemployment checks be mailed to Florida.

The war on unemployment is clearly being waged against an unspecified enemy, and the unemployment problem has long since outgrown its original definition.

In June of 1982, in the worst recession since the Great Depression, the figure was 9.6%. It broke down as follows:

1% were looking for work for the first time.

2.2% were re-entering the job market, having withdrawn for a while because they wanted to.

.7% had quit their jobs.

1.9% had been laid off temporarily.

3.8% had been fired.

So, only 60% of the unemployed had been laid off, and a third of those were waiting to be recalled. The rest would find jobs, on the average, in thirteen to fifteen weeks. Meanwhile, 40% were drawing unemployment insurance.

There are other distortions. For example, the figure includes a lot more teenagers than it did in the thirties, and a lot more women. Some women (not all, by any means) tend to move rather freely in and out of the labor force. If they don't find work as soon as they begin to look for it, they show up as unemployed. Some teenagers have to work. The money they earn keeps the family afloat. But large numbers of teenagers—many who live with well-to-do parents—work off and on to earn spending money. Whenever they're looking, they are officially unemployed. These two groups have probably inflated the figure a full percentage point.

Because it includes only persons who say they are looking for work, the figure excludes an unknown number who have given up. In so doing, it tends to ignore the men and women who most closely approach the thirties stereotype—the discouraged and the demoralized. As a measure of national distress, the official unemployment rate is worse than useless. Those who are suffering the most are omitted; those who are managing to get by will probably be counted.

The unemployment figure is based on a sample—60,000 households. One member is interviewed each month. The compilers of the figure readily concede that there is no way to tell how accurate the responses are. Anyone who tells a government pollster that he or she is out of a job and "looking for work" is automatically and uncritically included in the figure we look to as the measure of how well the economy is succeeding in what most people see as its primary task.

The unemployment figure can read just about what one wants it to. For example, if you want to limit it to persons who have been fired, it is 5.7%. If you want to limit it to those who have been out of work for more than fifteen weeks, it is 3.5%. If you want to limit it to men and women who have been unem-

ployed for twenty-six weeks or more, the rate is 1.7%—a figure
that would make no headlines and elect no congressman.

There is a more significant source of error. In recent years,
taxes and overregulation have driven an unknown and unknowable segment of the American economy underground.

In just one corner of this shadow economy, growing and
selling marijuana, one researcher estimates that the industry
employs as many as a million persons, 300,000 full-time. There
are California officials who predict that the value of marijuana
produced there may soon exceed the state's billion-dollar
grape industry. Hawaii may produce more marijuana than
sugar or pineapples. But the men and women who work in this
growth industry are not officially employed.

Unemployment is often aggravated by the government programs designed to reduce it. Just as one federal agency subsi-
dizes the production of tobacco while another agency tries to
restrict its use, some government programs promote the unemployment others struggle to prevent.

Unemployment insurance programs ignore those most in
need while artificially enlarging the pool of the jobless. Benefits can exceed 70% of prior earnings, and the difference in pay
for working as opposed to not working is often as little as 50
cents an hour. Experts who watch the work force are convinced that hundreds of thousands of men and women work
just long enough to qualify for benefits and then manage to be
laid off. Some economists estimate that the system may be
stretching spells of unemployment by as much as a third.

The minimum wage law is another major cause of unemployment. When, in 1976, Congress voted to increase the minimum wage from $2.30 to $3.35, the secretary of labor con-
ceded that the increase would disemploy enough teenagers to
fill the Los Angeles Coliseum.

The official unemployment figure has detached itself from
any solid reality. It doesn't mean what it used to mean. It
doesn't mean what most people probably think it means. It
probably doesn't mean much of anything at all. It mixes hard-

ship, inconvenience, and opportunism together in unknown proportions. This is not to say that unemployment is no longer a problem, only that we have no accurate indicator of its nature and extent, however much we pretend to.

The unemployment estimate is equally useless as an indicator of the overall health of the economy. It can go up when the economy is improving and down when it is weakening. Yet government pours billions of inflationary dollars into the economy whenever the unemployment figure exceeds some imagined intolerable level.

But the accurate measurement of unemployment is the least of the problem. By 1980, the therapy itself, so confidently adopted in 1946, had become discredited. On August 24 of that year, the Joint Economic Committee of Congress issued a statement flatly rejecting the premise that had guided public policy for more than a third of a century. It reviewed the six recessions since World War II and concluded that: "Government attempts to shorten the duration or reduce the intensity of recessions through countercyclical programs . . . have been ineffective." The report was all but unanimous: the committee's eight Republican members and eleven of twelve Democrats approved it.

Four years before, the committee report had expressed full confidence that the economy could be managed, and reproached the Ford administration for doubting it. "Administration officials," it said in an evident reference to the publication of *The General Theory* in 1936, "speak as though they had heard nothing of the progress [of the highly developed discipline of economics] in the past forty years." It sternly admonished the administration to "stop purveying ignorance." But what was reprehensible ignorance four years before had, by 1980, become the new economic wisdom.

The central proposition of the Keynesian model had been reduced to the idea that unemployment and inflation were locked into an iron, inverse relationship, like the two ends of a seesaw. This relationship was so fixed and predictable (if charted, it produced a clean, rising line called the Phillips Curve)* that it was a perfect instrument for policymaking.

And the assumption became so integral to public policy that in an alarming distortion of logic and language, policymakers began to speak of inflation as a "cure" for unemployment— and some still do. By one more twist of language we hear opponents of monetary expansion characterized as cruelly advocating recession as a cure for inflation.

But then, in the seventies, things began to go haywire. Stagnation and inflation appeared simultaneously, and the Keynesian edifice began to crumble. "The Keynesian conceptualization . . . is being torn to shreds," wrote a labor union economist.

Economist Paul Samuelson, who had been a central figure in the canonization of Keynes in the forties, confessed sheepishly that "experts feel less sure of their expertise."

James Callaghan, speaking as the British Labour Party's prime minister, said with a clarity rare in politics: "We used to think that you could just spend your way out of a recession and reduce unemployment by cutting taxes and boosting government spending . . . that option no longer exists . . . it only worked by injecting bigger doses of inflation into the economy followed by higher levels of unemployment as the next step. That is the history of the last twenty years."

And Charles L. Schultze, chairman of President Johnson's Council of Economic Advisors, echoed that conclusion precisely: "Every time we push the rate of unemployment toward acceptable low levels, by whatever means," he said, "we set off a new inflation. And, in turn, both the political and economic consequences of inflation make it impossible to achieve full employment."

Time has redeemed the critics of Keynes who warned that

---

* For Professor A. W. Phillips, an Australian economist, who first drew the curve in a celebrated article, "The Relation Between Unemployment and the Rate of Change of Money, Wage Rates in the United Kingdom, 1861–1957," which appeared in *Economica* in November 1958.

stimulation through spending would not create employment but only the illusion of it, and that in the long run such spending would itself become a principal cause of unemployment. It would seem to work only because its inflationary consequences would not at first be evident.

Inflation-induced employment is a mirage. Inflation distorts the signals that guide business decisionmaking. Inflation-induced price increases make undertakings appear profitable that in fact are not—encouraging a false, frantic activity that can only be sustained by more inflation.

Moreover, each infusion of inflation has less effect than the last. That is one reason inflation accelerates. Each new round of stimulation requires more inflation for the same effect, because protracted inflations build the expectation of still further inflation into the system. Interest rates go up because both borrowers and lenders expect prices to go up. Unions base their wage demands on the expectation of higher prices. Businessmen base their orders and inventories on the same expectation. Even a slowing down of inflation can trigger a recession. If the economy has come to expect an inflation rate of 12%, a reduction of the rate to 6% will produce a slowdown that invites the remedy of further inflation.

We have learned that in the long run inflation-producing deficits are not a cure for unemployment but a cause of it. At the same time, it has become clear that taxes and government borrowing are undermining the economy's ability to form jobs.

In the thirties, the economy was thought to be chronically overcapitalized. By the seventies, forty years of indifference to the need for capital had produced a staggering capital shortage. The Financial Executives Research Foundation estimates the gap between capital needs and probable savings in the 1980s at a trillion dollars, more or less, depending on rate of inflation.

By the eve of the 1980 election, excessive rates of taxation and regulation had driven perhaps a fifth of the economy underground in a national epidemic of civil disobedience. That vast, off-the-books, self-defined "enterprise zone" had grown larger than all but a few of the official economies of the world. The IRS now estimates the tax loss to be $95 billion a year, very roughly the amount of the 1982 deficit.

The part of the economy that had stayed above ground and borne the full force of taxation had without doubt been taxed so severely as to cripple its ability to pay taxes. (In 1939, less than 1% of the population paid income tax, and the total yield was $4.06 billion.) Fifty years after the Crash, the penalties on the savings and investment necessary to nourish business had become the highest in the industrialized world. The Depression madness of killing little pigs had evolved into a public policy that saw no limit to the taxes business would bear. Taxation had reduced our rate of saving to the lowest in the industrial world—by 1981, it had fallen below 5% (that year Japan's was 20%).

Real business earnings began to decline sharply in the mid-sixties. While earnings have increased in dollar terms, experts such as Harvard's Martin S. Feldstein, now chairman of the Council of Economic Advisors, believe that if business made proper allowance for the higher costs of replacing equipment and inventory, its earnings would be much, much lower— often even negative. In other words, although inflation itself obscured the reality, at least some corporations were, in effect, consuming capital—selling their tools to pay their taxes.

The rate at which government is pre-empting available credit has been increasing geometrically—more rapidly even than tax rates. In the fifties and sixties, government borrowed about 6% of the nation's lendable funds. In the seventies, that figure more than doubled to 14%. In 1980, the federal government borrowed $123 billion to cover its deficit and for its various loan programs—35% of the $348 billion raised that year in our credit markets. Like the tax rate, the rate of government pre-emption of the nation's credit has reached—and probably exceeded—the optimum rate in its own terms.

The policy-induced capital shortage (Keynes' euthanasia of

the rentier) hit small business, where the most new jobs are formed, the hardest.

MIT's Development Foundation compared the job-formation performance of eleven large companies over a five-year period. Six of the companies were seasoned giants with sales in the billions; five were newer companies built on recent technologies.

In the five years studied, the sales of the six older companies grew more than 10% a year to a total of $37 billion, but only 25,000 new jobs were formed. Although sales of the five young companies increased 40% a year, total sales were still less than a billion. But these five small companies formed 35,000 new jobs in five years—10,000 more than the six giants. A capital shortage means that as the competition for a dwindling supply of capital becomes more intense, smaller businesses like these tend to be crowded out first.

As capital investment dwindled, the United States' rate of productivity increase became the lowest in the industrialized world. Between 1948 and 1954, output per man hour increased 4% a year. Between 1956 and 1974, the rate of increase fell to 2.1%. In 1975, the figure became negative for the first time since it had been compiled.

The United States had become a disdeveloping nation. A third of a century of public responsibility for maintaining full employment had produced the kind of chronic stagnation it was designed to overcome.

In 1946, the federal government, confident that the means were at hand, had committed itself to guaranteeing a job for everyone. By 1982, while there was no very widely shared sense of an alternative, that immensely costly effort was acknowledged to be a dead end. Business failures reached a fifty-year high.

National policy toward unemployment, misguided by an exhausted method of measurement, has come full circle. Spending has become the cause of the conditions it sought to remedy. The cost of the programs intended to relieve unemployment by direct or indirect means has become a principal cause both of unemployment and inflation. Two-thirds of a national sample told *U.S. News & World Report* that full employment was no longer a realistic goal.

Opinion researcher Jay Schmeideskamp once told a reporter, "In our surveys, we ask people whether they think government economic policy is good, fair, or poor. Increasingly, the answer we get is just plain laughter."

8

The Rise and Fall of the Welfare State

"... it is characteristic of the mischiefs that arise from ... prodigality [in the public expenditure] that they creep onwards with a noiseless and stealthy step, that they commonly remain unseen and unfelt until they have reached a magnitude absolutely overwhelming."

William Gladstone
Four times Prime Minister of England

In 1950, four years after the Employment Act of 1946, Congress passed a law revising the social security program and increasing its benefits. The vote was overwhelmingly favorable: 81 to 2 in the Senate and 374 to 1 in the House. Yet, during the debate, a Senator wondered whether "any living man ... could tell exactly what is in the bill and how it will work out ... thirty years from now [that is to say, in 1980]."

In September 1950, I wrote an article, titled "Up the Welfare State," about the new law. I asked (too timidly, it seems to me now) whether Congress should have passed the bill without better answers to certain central questions, among them, "how much [the program] would cost and hence whether the nation could afford it, whether the trust fund conformed to actuarial principles, and, in any case, whether the government could be trusted with the money."

The cost projections for 1990 made at the time ranged from a low of $7.8 billion to a high of $11.7 billion, and one senator complained that the Senate was being asked "to enact legislation on a matter where estimates of cost vary as widely as

50%." "What," he said, "is the possible sense of making promises covering a period forty to fifty years hence, which may have to be fulfilled with crushing tax levies? How do we know that private business in 1990 or 2000 will be able to bear such a burden?"

Senator George of Georgia, then chairman of the Senate Finance Committee, said calmly that the committee, which recommended passage of the bill, was "not unconcerned with the eventual liability" but had "proceeded with faith in America to meet the problem."

As he signed the bill into law, President Truman said it was good but not enough.

In 1981, social security payments totaled $138 billion, more than 23% of the federal budget. When Roosevelt signed the original social security act in 1935, the maximum tax employees had to pay (and employers match) was $30 a year. It is now nearly $2000.

The program was in part a response to the popular Townsend Plan, under which any man or woman over sixty without a criminal record would receive $200 a month for life if he or she promised to spend the money during the month it was received.

At first the Roosevelt administration called the plan "cockeyed," but in 1934, the president said, "Congress can't stand the pressure of the Townsend Plan unless we have a real old-age insurance system, nor can I face the country...."

What began as a program to provide a floor of protection under the neediest workers has become an immense web that involves nearly every American. There are 36 million beneficiaries, and more than 115 million employees are paying into the system.

In 1965, after a long, fractious debate, a medical program (Medicare) was added. By 1980 there were 28 million beneficiaries.

As the program grew and taxes increased, social security seemed to be choking the growth of private pension plans. Private pension coverage increased rapidly in the early years:

between 1940 and 1950 coverage doubled to 21%. In the fifties it doubled again. Then, in the sixties, it began to grow more slowly. By 1980 private pension coverage had reached only 50% of the work force. Now it's growing at only a third of a percent a year.

Although there was always talk of a trust fund, the social security program was never funded in the sense of having enough money put aside to pay its eventual obligations. If that had been done, there would now be a huge balance, out of which the system would be paying its current beneficiaries. But there is no balance. The taxes the system receives (even at today's high rate) are barely enough to pay its current obligations. · The program's unfunded net liability is now $4 trillion—or 4000 billion dollars.

An economist calculated in 1982 that America's capital investment was a trillion dollars less than it would have been had private, funded plans been somehow substituted for social security.

The system is a time bomb. As the eighties began, the taxes of 3.3 workers were available for each retiree. But that ratio is declining. In less than thirty years, in 2010, when the war babies reach sixty-five, there will be only two workers to support each retiree. Long before that, the system's politics will collide with its economics. It can be made to work on paper only by cutting benefits or raising taxes—courses that are barely conceivable politically.

Government employees, for whom the system is optional, are voting to withdraw by the tens of thousands. A *Times*/CBS poll in 1981 estimated that more than half the population was losing confidence in the social security system; that 54% doubt they'll get the pensions they're paying for. The government had made promises it could not withdraw and could not keep.

The overall growth of the federal government, obscured until recently from the public consciousness, can be quickly summarized. Before 1930, its domestic spending was never more than a billion dollars annually. During the seven years of the New Deal, outlays for peaceful purposes never exceeded $7 billion. By 1952, they had reached $12 billion. When Professor Galbraith wrote *The Affluent Society* in 1958, suggesting we were starving the public sector, the federal budget was $70 billion. Total spending reached $100 billion for the first time in 1962, 173 years after the Republic was formed. In 1971, it was $200 billion. Six years after that, in 1977, it exceeded $400 billion. In 1983 it will probably exceed $800 billion.

And these totals ignore two categories of federal spending that are half-hidden—off-budget programs and the net cost of government-sponsored enterprises—which will almost double the 1981 on-budget deficit. According to the House Budget Committee, "there appears to be no clear or consistent distinction between on- and off-budget entities." Off-budget programs cost a mere one-tenth of a billion in 1973. In 1980 they cost about $23 billion. Government-sponsored enterprises, mostly loan or loan-guarantee programs, added another $23 billion to the 1981 deficit.

Newsweek was nearly hysterical. "Federal spending is running wildly out of control," it said in a news story that read like a *Daily News* editorial. "Like some crazed creature from a science-fiction fantasy, the already bloated budget continues to balloon, feeding on the very mechanisms that are supposed to govern it and smothering growth in other sectors of the economy. The figures are staggering."

The federal debt, which represents simply the government's accumulated deficits, now exceeds a trillion dollars.

And overhanging all this (and aside from the gigantic unfunded liability of the social security program) are the huge contingent liabilities of federal insurance and loan-gaurantee programs, which now total $2.3 trillion.

We are told that federal civilian employment leveled off years ago at about 2.9 million. But the *National Journal* believes there are another 9 million "invisible employees" paid "either directly by the federal government or indirectly through intermediaries."

The independent sector has been largely pushed aside and forgotten. We have no reliable sense of the full dimensions of that sector, but in 1981, reported money contributions to its most visible institutions totaled $54 billion, or 2% of the gross national product.

The government has long since abandoned any pretense of limiting its largesse to the distressed or disadvantaged. By the mid-seventies, the welfare state had become the full-service state. Federally subsidized student loans were available to all, regardless of income. Farm subsidies and low-interest REA loans sustained millionaires. Midway in the Reagan administration, families with incomes over $75,000 could still qualify for interest-subsidized student loans. The services the FAA provides owners of private planes costs to $3600 per plane per year.

The Institute for Socioeconomic Studies recently counted 182 distinct federal "transfer payment" programs—ones that make direct payments in cash or kind to individuals. They include social security at one end of the scale and indemnity payments to beekeepers on the other.

In 1950, there were five people working in the private economy for each transfer payment recipient. By 1981, this ratio had declined to 1.3 to 1.

In spring 1981, the Census Bureau reported that 39.5% of the households receiving food stamps were not "poor," as it is officially defined. (About three-fourths of England's population lives below our poverty line.) Neither were 57.3% of the households getting subsidized school lunches, 53.4% of those in subsidized housing, 52.5% of those covered by Medicaid, and 82% of those covered by Medicare. Conversely, two-thirds of the officially designated "poor" received no cash benefits, and almost three-fifths received no noncash benefits.

There was no longer any apparent limit to the scope of the federal government: it had, in half a century, achieved a near monopoly of the public business.

The abiding impulse to regulate the economy has exploded

as well. As Galbraith told an interviewer, "The nice thing about capitalism is that it lends itself to an infinity of patching up."

In 1929, there were twelve federal regulatory agencies; the New Deal added eleven. But twenty, nearly twice as many, were born in the seventies. The cost of regulation increased fivefold in that decade, from $1.2 billion in 1971 to $6 billion in 1980. The Code of Federal Regulations was 77,498 pages long. That year there were 40,000 lawyers practicing in Washington.

The Carter administration issued 7192 new regulations during its last year. The Reagan administration reduced the rate of growth somewhat, but nontheless issued 5648 new regulations during its first year.

We are astounded to read that it required more than 2000 pages to print the regulations governing calico factories in mercantilist France. But the Council on Wage and Price Stability recently listed 5600 separate regulations to which the steel industry must comply.

And while the president's economic advisers were debating whether to declare a state of economic emergency, the U.S. Customs Service was pondering whether or not to reclassify Burberry trenchcoats as "ornamented garments" because they have epaulets. Officials at the Department of Health, Education and Welfare were dealing with complaints that a school regulation requiring girls to wear brassieres was discriminatory under the law unless boys were required to wear them too.

The thirties and forties produced a large, ardent literature that imagined the boundless possibilities of activist government. The sixties and seventies produced a literature of a different sort—sadder, saner chronicles of the failures of intervention.

Many of the authors of these revisionist studies, although by no means all of them, were intellectuals who had once favored "liberal" programs (a term which, regrettably, for fifty years could mean only government programs) in the abstract, but who found the reality disappointing. They became the born-again conservatives—the neoconservatives. They were liberals, Irving Kristol said, who had been mugged by reality.

One by one, disillusioned liberals defected, wrote a penitential monograph about how this or that promising federal program had failed in practice, until their ranks were so nearly emptied of objectivity and common sense that one of their number was moved to call for a new, "rational" liberalism to repair the damage.

The production of these confessions soon became a thriving industry. One of the first was called *The Federal Bulldozer*, by Martin Anderson, who was then at Columbia. Published in 1964, Anderson's study demonstrated that the federal housing programs had destroyed more homes than they had built. The study became a sort of model. A half-dozen neoconservative research centers began turning out these exposés, first in a trickle and then in a torrent. It was computerized muckraking on a grand scale. Now the literature documenting the failure of federal action has become almost as immense and impenetrable as government itself.

With its lingering descriptions of unspeakable extravagance and its delicious close-ups of billion-dollar perversities, this new literature is the pornography of the social sciences. But, like pornography, in the end it is boring, as the same sorry obscenities are repeated with endless, necessarily minor variations.

The costly farm programs ignore the marginal farmers they were designed to help. They also pay farmers not to plant on land they wouldn't plant on anyway. Social security is a disaster from every point of view. Participants could buy equal, more secure protection from private companies for much less money. In case after case, regulation originally designed to protect consumers from predatory producers has in practice protected producers from competition. Foreign "aid" has slowed the growth of poor nations. A team of scholars concluded that, "If the goal of the medical-care delivery system is the improvement of health, a good deal of money has been spent to no discernible effect." Drug regulation has stifled research on lifesaving medicines.

Economist Thomas Sowell summarized the intricate incompetence of the poverty programs: "The total amount of money the government spends on its many antipoverty efforts is three times what would be required to lift every man, woman and child in America above the official poverty line by simply sending money to the poor."

Studies like these were the full-length features of fiscal pornography. There were also the quickies—the fillers and tailpieces in the *Reader's Digest* and *The Rotarian*, the three-for-a-quarter peep-show glimpses of the unnatural acts of naked government: The twelve-member Franklin Delano Roosevelt Memorial Commission, established in 1955, has spent more than $400,000 searching without success for a suitable monument to a president who said he didn't want one. The Pentagon publishes 371 separate periodicals. Federal employees in a Manhattan office spend $3000 a month calling Dial-a-Joke. In 1982, the Post Office issued a 300-page plan for continued mail deliveries after an atomic attack.

Research is a tantalizing subcategory of obscene silliness: $200,000 to study speech patterns in Philadelphia; $50,000 to create a taste for chili in rats; $27,000 to find out why inmates want to escape from prison. The Department of Agriculture spent $113,417 asking 2161 women if they preferred children's clothing that didn't require ironing.

What has come to pass has fulfilled not the ebullient prophecies of the architects of the new day, but the more doleful ones of its critics.

We are rediscovering an ancient perception—that there are natural limits to most methods of government finance . . . except currency inflation. Confucius was once a tax collector, his task made more difficult by the fact that the ruler had just increased to one-fifth his levy on what the nation produced. People had believed for years that one-tenth was a fair and reasonable tribute for the governed to pay; many flatly refused to pay the increase. Gibbon quoted an eighteenth-century maxim that "no State, without soon being exhausted" could keep more than one percent of the population in "arms and idleness"—about 2½% of the labor force.

Taxation is, of course, not the only resource available to the modern state. It can borrow. It can spend money earmarked for other purposes—in effect, borrowing from itself. And, in what amounts to the same thing, it can temporarily put off spending for purposes popularly considered indispensable.

But now all these methods of paying for governmental growth have, almost suddenly and simultaneously, reached their limits. Taxation has not only reached its limits of growth, it has probably exceeded them.

There are clearly limits to what government can borrow without destroying the private economy's ability to lend, as its pre-emption of lendable funds drives interest rates to destructive levels.

"There is no room between Scylla and Charybdis," a Federal Reserve governor told a reporter, while asking for anonymity. "You can push the economy so hard [into recession] to kill inflation that . . . there is no investment. So you get the anti-inflation effects but not any expansionary effects and if you ease you get the inflation again. Whether you eased or you didn't, no one is a winner."

When the government collects special taxes earmarked for special purposes—the social security trust fund, the highway trust fund, the unemployment-insurance trust fund—it spends the money immediately and puts federal promises to pay into the "funds." These funds now "own" over $200 billion of the federal debt. The budget tactfully calls these holdings "investments." For years—as long as the current receipts of these funds far exceeded the outgo—this was the simplest way to finance part of the deficit. But now these programs—social security is overwhelmingly the largest—are beginning to pay out more than they take in. (In the case of social security, its outgo is expected to exceed its income by $63.5 billion in 1986.) What in the past served to artificially ease the fiscal squeeze will now intensify it.

For twenty-five years before 1980, potential deficits were somewhat reduced as military spending decreased as a percent of GNP. Between 1954 and 1979, nonmilitary spending more than doubled, from 7.8% of the GNP to 15.9%, while military spending fell by half, from 11.5% of the GNP to 5.0%. During that period the Soviet Union continued to increase the rate of its military spending as ours declined. By 1980, leaders of both major political parties, alarmed by the resulting imbalance, were saying that military spending should be sharply increased for a period of five years. The opinion polls showed a very high degree of public accord.

Now there is a growing dissent from that view, as military and fiscal considerations have become hopelessly intermingled. But however these fiscal and military considerations are compromised, the present fiscal crisis did not develop during a period of increasing military spending, but during a period of substantial decline in such spending. Any fiscal relief achieved by reduced spending for weapons can only be temporary.

After fifty years of unrestrained government growth, the United States is bankrupt in the only sense in which a government with the power to print money can be said to be bankrupt. It has used up all the forms of financing further growth except inflation. It can tax no more; it can only reshape the pattern of taxation to try to make it more efficient. It cannot increase the share of the nation's credit it devours. There are no more substantial special-fund balances. It can no longer spend much more for welfare by spending much less for weapons.

As government continues to grow, it will inevitably resort with less and less restraint to a method it knows well—direct increases in the money supply: the monetary equivalent of mainlining. By 1982, it was evident that the Reagan administration, partly out of innocence and partly by intent, had made inflationary financing the centerpiece of its domestic policy.

In 1945, an Australian economist named Colin Clark, a pleasant, blunt iconoclast whose mind never stopped working, contended in an article in *The Economic Journal* that once the cost of government consumes as much as 25% of a nation's income, currency devaluation (inflation) becomes inevitable because the citizens simply refuse to tolerate higher taxes. Clark's colleagues, mostly keen new converts to Keynesian economics, jumped all over him for trying to spoil the fun, but now Clark's rule of thumb is being mentioned again and has the ring of prophecy.

"Once taxation has exceeded 25% of the national income," Clark wrote, "influential sections of the community become willing to support a depreciation of the value of money; while so long as taxation remains below this critical limit, the balance of forces favours a stable, or occasionally an increasing, value of money." These "influential sections" have appeared among us as the supply-side economists who plausibly advocate tax cuts to stimulate the growth of the private sector, regardless of inflationary consequences.

Clark acknowledged that in the United States the percentage might be higher, and, undoubtedly, for better or for worse, our tolerance for taxation is the world's highest. But there is still a "critical limit" and almost certainly we have already exceeded it.

In 1975, an English professor of economics, Harry Johnson, echoed Colin Clark's warning: ". . . inflation is likely to become chronic when government expenditure surpasses a certain relative size, at which point the public becomes unwilling to pay in taxation for the government services it votes for and is accustomed to."

The supply-side program, which calls for large across-the-board cuts in marginal tax rates, carries an anti-inflationary banner. Martin Anderson, Reagan's chief economic adviser during the campaign, wrote in a policy memo in August of 1979:

1. Inflation is the main domestic problem facing the United States today. . . .
2. The main cause of inflation is the massive, continuing budget deficit of the federal government.
3. The most effective way to eliminate the deficit is to reduce the rate of growth of federal expenditures and to simultaneously stimulate the economy so as to increase revenues in such a way that the private share grows proportionately more than the government share. . . .

In less than two years, this administration produced the largest deficit in American history. Advocates of what came to be called Reaganomics may have believed their hopeful projections proving that a more carefully taxed private sector would become so productive that it would keep pace with the government's awesome appetite for resources. But they believed more surely that, if government growth proved uncontrollable, inflation would be a better way to finance it than direct taxation. George Gilder's *Wealth and Poverty* says it clearly: government will continue to grow "even if the gargantuan waste and perversity of leftist giveaways decline. But even if Congress manages to pass the usual boondoggles, we should not abandon the drive to retrench taxes. . . . In an economy with an overweening public sector, deficit spending, even in substantial amounts, is decidedly preferable to tax increases." And a page later, he states the case unmistakably: "Deficit spending can be a way of protecting the private sector and its most catalytic investments from the effects of direct taxes."

And thus is Clark's prophecy fulfilled. Inflation is advocated as preferable to direct taxation by a group of vastly influential policymakers who won public support with promises to stop inflation. One can imagine a Huey Long interview: "Senator, do you think hyperinflation will ever come to this country?" "Sure," Huey replies, "but here we'll call it inflation control."

The Reagan administration marked the end of an era, but it was not the one most pundits meant. It did not signal the end of expanding government, it meant the end of an era of pretense that government spending could be controlled. It meant that the more conservative of the major political parties could hope only to control the *rate* of growth somewhat.

The election of 1980 began a period in which the responsibilities of government were sure to grow faster than the resources available to pay for them, one in which the difference would be paid for by monetizing debt.

For twenty years, every administration had sanctioned the emergency use of inflation. The Reagan administration institutionalized it.

Since 1960, the government has issued about $100 billion in new money—Federal Reserve notes created to buy the Treasury's promises to pay. This figure is not hard to locate. The wonder is that the press has not reported its steady and ominous increase as noisily as it reports the endless hopeful predictions of budget surpluses that somehow are never realized.

Each year's budget reports on the federal debt according to who holds it. As of September 30, 1981, it totaled a trillion dollars; $670 billion is said to exist outside the Federal Reserve System, which means that the Treasury had borrowed money that already had existed. And $124 billion is said to be held by the Federal Reserve System, meaning money that had been created so that the government could borrow it. (Another $209 billion was borrowed from various trust funds.)

Then the process thickens. Money so created disproportionately enlarges the overall supply of money and credit as banks issue credit in excess of cash reserves. There is a connection, but because the Federal Reserve has discretion as to how much credit a given quantity of Federal Reserve notes will support, it is not a mechanical one. Between 1960 and 1981, for example, the Federal Reserve holdings of government debt increased from $26 billion to $124 billion, an increase of $98 billion. In those twenty-one years, the basic money supply, officially called M1, increased from $141 billion to $440 billion, an increase of 213%. During those years, the price level, as measured by the consumer price index, moved from 89 to 285, an increase of 220%.

We are in dangerous territory, for in circumstances such as these, inflation will eventually prevail. No society has ever taxed itself to death, but inflation is in effect a sort of tax—one that is impossible to circumvent. When a government monetizes its debt, it taxes its citizens just as surely as if it had imposed a sales tax or capital levy. The government gains purchasing power; the public loses it, the reduction taking the form of reductions in the value of cash holdings. Inflation is a tax on money.

In the Great German Inflation of the twenties, Berliners were paid every day at noon. When, instead of eating lunch, they sprinted to the nearest shop to buy *anything*—from cuckoo clocks to shoes that didn't fit—before their money lost more of its value, they were racing to escape taxation. People fight visible taxes fiercely or refuse to pay them. When, as the German inflation accelerated, the leader of the Center Party suggested tax increases as an alternative to more inflation, someone tried to kill him. But inflation is an invisible, inescapable tax, one that can be levied without the approval of the legislature. You can suggest some plausible generalizations about who pays inflationary taxes, but you cannot prove them. It amounts to a cruel, clandestine, and arbitrary form of taxation that only theoretically involves representation. It is an especially dangerous form of taxation, for there are no restraints on its irresponsible use. And the end result is not just a chastened and disappointed society but a demolished one.

9

The Death of the Dollar

"Once the deficit has become the dominating feature of the situation and has reached a figure of many millions, all saving of small amounts seems useless; it is believed that only great reforms could afford salvation; and the financial administration is possessed by a spirit of dissipation and neglect."

Constantino Bresciani-Turroni
The Economics of Inflation

In the midst of Germany's great inflation, a few months before the final explosion in November 1923, Dr. Rudolf Havenstein, head of the Reichsbank, was describing to the Reichstag the bank's strenuous efforts to supply what he called "the vastly increased demand for the means of payment." The bank was first of all, he said, providing simpler banknotes of larger and larger denominations. Thirty-one mills were producing the paper and a hundred private printers were working around the clock to supplement the bank's own presses. Still, he continued, "the running of the Reichbank's note printing organization, which has become absolutely enormous, is making the most extreme demands on our personnel. The dispatching of cash sums must, for reasons of speed, be made by private transport. Numerous shipments leave Berlin every day for the provinces. The deliveries to several banks can be made . . . only by airplanes."

Privately, Havenstein confided to an economist friend that he needed a new suit, but he was going to wait till prices came down to buy one.

The world's inflationary experience varies in particulars, but there is an unmistakable common root: Inflation is an alter-

native to direct taxation and borrowing. Governments inflate
when the costs of some irresistible obligation—war or a social
vision pursued with a warlike intensity—outrun the ability to
tax and borrow.

Runaway inflations are common in history. They have taken
place in nations where the people were sane and civilized.
They have been carefully dissected and analyzed. All of history's runaway inflations originated in some perceived necessity and grew in a vacuum of uncertainty about how money
works. All, however idiotic they seem in retrospect, had a
widely supported rationale and a powerful and persuasive constituency.

The most famous of all, the Great German Inflation, began
in 1914 when Germany, fighting a war it was sure it would
win, suspended gold payments and began to print money to
pay the costs.

It was inconceivable to the participants that a war fought
with dreadful weapons such as airplanes, long-range cannon,
and poison gas could last more than a few months. And Karl
Helfferich, Germany's treasury secretary, told the Reichstag,
"After the war . . . our enemies shall make restitution for all
the material damage . . . they have caused by the irresponsible
launching of the war against us." Thus Germany relied much
less on taxation and borrowing from the public than did the
Allies. Between 1914 and 1918, Germany spent 164 billion
marks. Only 23 billion (14%) was raised by taxation (at that
time taxing power resided primarily in the German states); 98
billion was borrowed; and the rest, about 43 billion, took the
form of Treasury bills. Half of these bills, discounted at the
Reichsbank, became monetized debt.

After defeat, the government continued to spend heavily—
not just for the enormous reparations imposed by the Allies but
also to pay for demobilization and the expenses that accompa-
nied the national turmoil as the Kaiser's Germany collapsed.

The short-lived Weimar Republic, organized in the national
theater in that historic city, was, from the start, beset by famine, unemployment, and its own clumsy inexperience. Lord

Keynes, in Berlin with three other economists, pleaded in vain that Germany balance the budget, stabilize the mark, and stop printing money.

By 1920, inflation was moving out of control. A final effort was made to increase taxes, but spending grew even faster, and taxes were meeting only 40% of government costs. The money supply continued its steep climb. The socialists pressed for higher taxes, including a capital levy, while the conservative parties, fiercely opposed to socialism, were less concerned about deficits.

By the summer of 1922, the inflationary circle had closed. The government's need for money increased as the real value of money declined—budget estimates became obsolete before the Reichstag had time to ratify them—and the final geometric increases in note issue began. Capital flight and the annihilation of wealth eroded the tax base and reduced still further the tax-supported share of spending. In October 1923, taxes paid less than 1% of the cost of government. All the rest was financed by fiat money.

Then the last acceleration began. By November 20, the rate of the mark to the dollar was 11.7 trillion to one. The call loan rate reached 10,950%. The German mark was dead.

The idea that the "so-called inflation" of the money supply had no connection with soaring prices persisted throughout the German catastrophe with a tenacity that is, from this distance, incredible. Adolph Lowe, a young official in the German Economics Ministry at the time, says ". . . the general theory in Germany then was that prices rose or fell by themselves, and the government had to adjust the amount of money to provide what was needed to satisfy the demand for money."

Most economists denied a connection between money and prices, preferring a "sociological" concept of money that viewed changes in the value of money as an "historical process."

A German economic journal complained in 1922 that the Allied press was forever "accusing Germany of ruining her exchange with gigantic note issues," when in fact "everyone in

Germany knows that for months already the note issues of the
Reichsbank have been nominally most gigantic, but actually
they are small, very small, if account is taken of their real
value."

Almost until the final debacle, many industrialists contended
that the depreciation of the currency was good for business; it
encouraged exports and tourism and stimulated domestic demand. They warned against the hazards of stabilization. "Any
further improvement in the mark," one said, "would paralyze
exports and provoke vast unemployment."

"I informed the gentlemen," Hugo Stinnes* wrote in a
memorandum describing a conversation with a group of foreign diplomats, "that the weapon of inflation would have to be
used in the future . . . because only that made it possible to
give the population orderly and regular activity which was
necessary to preserve the life of the nation."

America's first great inflation, the byproduct of revolution,
grew out of circumstances strikingly similar to Weimar Germany's. Less than a week after the battle of Bunker Hill, the
Continental Congress, lacking the power to tax, issued $2 mil-
lion in paper notes and hired twenty-eight men to sign them.
Before the war was won, at least $240 million had been is-
sued—possibly more in secret. The colonies issued another
$200 million of their own. Congress declared the notes legal
tender and branded anyone who refused them "an enemy of
the country."

The Continental currency began to depreciate rapidly in
1779. By 1781, it had lost 99% of its value. Within a few
months it was worthless. Barbers papered their shops with the
notes. Sailors who, after bitter months at sea, were paid off
with unspendable notes, had suits of clothes made from them.
The notes were called "shinplasters," and their issue was
called "shinning."

* The legendary Hugo Stinnes, who seemed to believe the inflation would go
on forever, bought 2000 companies on credit which he paid off in depreciated
marks. He ran his empire by telephone as he traveled in search of new acquisi-
tions, his records on scraps of paper he kept in his pockets, like the boy tycoon in
William Gaddis' *JR*.

Thomas Jefferson estimated that the issues amounted to an arbitrary confiscation of $36 million of the property of American people. The losses were distributed at random as the depreciating currency was passed from hand to hand like the Old Maid in the children's card game. Peletiah Webster, who has been called the first great American economist, and who strongly opposed the printing of the Continental currency, wrote soon after, "Paper money polluted the equity of our laws, turned them into engines of oppression, corrupted the justice of our public administration, destroyed the fortunes of thousands who had confidence in it, enervated the trade, husbandry and manufactures of our country, and went far to destroy the morality of our people."

During the Civil War, the North, which chose to tax, escaped hyperinflation, and the South, which elected to inflate its currency, did not. When the first shots were fired at Fort Sumter, both sides believed the contest would be over in a few months. Enlistments were for ninety days, and Washington hesitated to use taxes to pay for the war. The first year, the North set out to borrow a quarter of a billion dollars. Secretary of the Treasury Chase said solemnly that the greatest care would be taken to "prevent a degradation of such issues into an irredeemable paper currency, than which no more certainly fatal expedient for impoverishing the masses and discrediting the government of any country can well be devised."

But as the war dragged on and the costs mounted, borrowing these huge sums became difficult. Lincoln's government suspended gold payments in December 1861, and a month later Congress began an historic debate on meeting deficits by issuing greenbacks—irredeemable, unsecured notes made legal tender by fiat. Congressman Justin S. Morrill was aghast. "If it be a war measure," he thundered, "it . . . will be of greater advantage to the enemy. I would as soon provide Chinese wooden guns for the army as paper money." The defenders of the greenbacks said only that they were a desperate, distasteful necessity. There was no alternative. "Rather than yield to revolutionary force," Senator John Sherman told his colleagues, "I would use a revolutionary force."

The resistance collapsed after the first debate. Six hundred million dollars was issued altogether, but these issues totaled less than a fifth of the cost of government during the war years. Americans showed an eagerness to pay taxes which dumfounded observers from abroad. "I was not surprised," one foreign minister said, "to see your young men rushing enthusiastically to fight for their flag. . . . But I have never before seen a country where people were clamorous for taxation." The results of the Union inflation were serious but manageable. Prices doubled during the four war years, but the United States resumed gold payments in 1879.

In the South, of course, it was different. By the time Robert E. Lee surrendered at Appomattox, prices had increased 9200%, for the Confederacy, with no tax-collecting authority or machinery, had printed most of the money it spent for war. By July 1863 there were 262 note-signers in the Confederate Treasury Department. There was a shortage of paper and printers, and for a while the Confederacy collected counterfeit money, stamped it "valid," and put it back into circulation. William McCormick, in a letter to his brother Cyrus in England, described creditors running away from their debtors, who "pursued them in triumph and paid them without mercy."

While the Yankees were clamoring to pay taxes, tax resistance in the Confederacy stiffened: "We of today are paying the price of our righteous war in blood," said the *Wilmington Journal*. "It is but just and right that posterity should pay in money. . . . Let our authorities then fearlessly . . . stretch the public credit to the utmost . . . so that taxation may not crush to earth our already overburdened people." That hyperinflation, the effects lost in the larger turmoil of defeat, was the last in American history.

But elsewhere, the practice of resorting to the printing press when, for a variety of reasons, taxes and borrowing prove insufficient to finance some "uncontrollable" government obligation, has recurred dozens of times. Poland's inflation after World War I was the result of a proud national tradition·of tax resistance. Before the war, the Polish tax system had been administered by Russia, Germany, and Austria-Hungary, and the subject Poles had evaded taxes as an expression of patriotism. When, after the war, Warsaw set up its own taxing apparatus, this tradition compounded the problems of an inexperienced bureaucracy, and the Polish government began to print much of the money it needed to pay the costs of reconstruction. In the last year of the resulting inflation, prices increased by a factor of 699.

Russia spent 67 billion rubles fighting World War I and recovered only a fourth of that in taxes. Between 1913 and 1921, the Russian price level increased 4900000%.

The Hungarian inflation after World War II, one of the maddest of all, was triggered by the Nazi theft of that nation's gold reserves. At the peak, it took 828 octillians of paper Hungarian pengoes to equal one pre-war pengo. History's largest-denomination banknote was issued then for one hundred million billion pengoes. It was worth about a nickel.

In more recent years, there was the classic case of Allende's Chile. The Marxist government instituted expensive programs for which a congress dominated by opposition parties refused to levy taxes. As a result, in 1970, the government deficit was 2.3 billion escudas, and much of it was monetized. In 1971, the deficit was 8.4 billion; in 1972, 10 billion; and in 1973, 12.3 billion. In 1971, the money supply increased 113%; in 1972, 151%; and in 1973 nearly 500%. During that period, the price level increased more than 2500%.

There is no iron law of economics stipulating that every protracted inflation sooner or later goes out of control. But history's runaway inflations reveal, in grotesque magnification, what happens to a democratic society when its government's obligations exceed its economic strength.

The universal image of runaway inflation is that of a Berliner pushing a wheelbarrowful of money down Unter den Linden to buy a cabbage or a newspaper. Or the German housewife who leaves a basketful of money for a minute and, returning, finds the money safe and the basket stolen. Moderate inflation is a serious economic problem. Runaway inflation is a bad joke—something freakish and exceptional, beyond the pale of legitimate human experience, the sort of thing Ripley used to put in his "Believe It or Not" features along with two-headed calves and flagpole sitters. The human consequences, of course, are not funny.

In the fall of 1923, Maximillian Bern, an aging German anthologist, withdrew his life savings from his Berlin bank, spent it all for a subway ticket for a last ride around the city, returned to his apartment, locked the door, and starved to death.

In those last terrible days of Germany's Great Inflation, the mark was losing its value by the hour. There was a mad daily scrimmage for anything tangible. People quickly learned not to hold cash a minute longer than they had to. Artur Schnabel was paid for a concert with a suitcaseful of banknotes so heavy he needed help to carry it. On the way home, to lighten the load, he spent half his fee for two sausages. A German student remembers that the price of a cup of coffee went up from 5000 to 8000 marks while he was drinking it.

By November 1923, a single match cost 900 million marks, a kilo of bread was 428 billion marks, a bus ticket 150 billion, and a stamp for a domestic letter 100 billion.

When László Moholy-Nagy, the Bauhaus artist, could no longer afford paint and canvas, he created his famous "Bankruptcy Vultures" collage with worthless currency. Constantino Bresciani-Turroni, author of the definitive history of the Great German Inflation, wrote: "Inflation dispensed its favors blindly, and often the least meritorious enjoyed them." Thomas Mann's old governess proudly told the family she would soon retire and live on what she'd saved. But the thousands she'd carefully put away over the years—a few marks at a time—were then worth less than a penny. Once-wealthy people sold first their furniture and then their art treasures: they might live for a few weeks on the price of a Rembrandt. Families kept pigs in the pantry or raised chickens in their gardens.

A German woman remembers: "My father had taken out endowment insurance ... calculated to cover my brothers' [and my] university education. ... When my eldest brother got his money it was just sufficient to buy a bicycle. When the second got his, he could just buy a pair of boots. When my turn came I got nothing."

Money that middle-class people had saved for their daughters' dowries dissolved and with it Germany's marriage customs. Chastity was the fashion before the Great Inflation, but after the war Berliners liked to say that the stone lions at the foot of Unter den Linden would roar if a virgin walked by. Adolescent prostitutes were popular, and the older women solicited in little-girl makeup. Berlin became Babylon, and cocaine its favorite drug.

"When I grew up," a German who was a child during the Great Inflation remembers, "we were taught to save money and not to throw it away. ... But in the worst days of the Inflation this principle was turned upside down. We knew that to hold on to money was the worst thing we could do."

The streets were unsafe. People shot aimlessly at passersby. "But I thought it was a big pigeon," one sniper told the police. People stole leather window straps from railway cars and siphoned gas from unwatched cars.

For millions, the inflation was an unspeakable hardship. In 1923, 5,632,000 Germans were on relief. The poorest ate dog meat. The Ministry of the Interior approved the use of cheap cardboard coffins.

Fortunes were made as inadvertently and arbitrarily as others were lost. Foreign students, whose modest allowances were paid in hard currencies, bought whole blocks of abandoned houses.

Hotel porters, who received tips in foreign currency, prospered. A countess rented her house to Americans for a few dollars and moved into the attic. Apartment owners paid off mortgages with depreciated marks, but in time rent control and tenure laws made the properties worthless. Toward the end vandals stole doorknobs and light fixtures, and even the lead sheets on the roofs and metal number plates.

Inflation became the central concern of everyone's life. Thomas Mann's little daughter chanted, "The dollar is up," each time the head of her rocking horse rose. There was a great increase in speculative experts: dealers, agents, middlemen, and all kinds of "consultants" who advised the bewildered population in the unfamiliar business of salvaging something from the inflationary hurricane. More than 400 new banks were formed in 1923.

Bresciani-Turroni writes: "The number of middlemen increased continually at a time when the buying and selling of goods, thanks to the very rapid increase in prices, created the possibility of quick profits. Besides legitimate commerce, which already included a very long chain of middlemen, there grew and blossomed in the hothouse of the currency depreciation clandestine commerce, which was devoted to bargaining in all sorts of foodstuffs, useful articles, artistic objects, gold and silver goods, etc."

The number of bankruptcies fell from 815 a month in 1913 to a mere eight in November 1923, as the distinction between sound and unsound economic activity disappeared in the confusion. Inflation had paralyzed the invisible hand.

Although inflation is an economic phenomenon, its most profound and permanent consequences go far beyond economics. Runaway inflations leave nations limp and helpless. They are the social equivalent of holocaust. Societies have endured recessions—however battered and altered—with their essentials intact, but they have not usually survived runaway inflations.

Leopold Ullstein said of the Weimar inflation, "There was a feeling of utter dependence on anonymous powers—almost as a primitive people believe in magic—that somebody must be in the know, and that this small group of somebodies must be a conspiracy." In April 1923, young Adolf Hitler told a Munich audience, "The first thing we must do is rescue [Germany] from the Jew who is ruining our country."

Historian Alan Bullock wrote later: "The collapse of the currency not only meant the end of trade, bankrupt businesses, food shortages in the big cities and unemployment. It had the effect, which is the unique quality of economic catastrophe, of reaching down to and touching every single member of the community in a way which no political event can. The savings of the middle classes and the working classes were wiped out at a single blow with a ruthlessness which no revolution could ever equal. . . . The result of the inflation was to undermine the foundations of German society in a way which neither the war, nor the revolution of November, 1918, nor the Treaty of Versailles had ever done. The real revolution was the inflation."

A severe inflation, Mann wrote, "is the worst kind of revolution. . . . There is neither system nor justice in the expropriation and redistribution of property resulting from inflation. A cynical 'each man for himself' becomes the rule of life. But only the most powerful, the most resourceful and unscrupulous, the hyenas of economic life, can come through unscathed. The great mass of those who put their trust in the traditional order, the innocent and unworldly, all those who do productive and useful work, but don't know how to manipulate money, the elderly who hoped to live on what they earned in the past—all these are doomed to suffer. . . .

"A straight line runs from the madness of the German Inflation to the madness of the Third Reich . . . the market woman who without batting an eyelash demanded a hundred million for an egg, lost the capacity for surprise. And nothing that has happened since has been insane or cruel enough to surprise her.

"It was during the Inflation that the Germans forgot how to rely on themselves as individuals and learned to expect every-

thing from 'politics,' from the 'state,' from 'destiny.' They
learned to look on life as a wild adventure, the outcome of
which depended not on their own effort but on sinister, myste-
rious forces. The millions who were . . . robbed of their wages
and savings became the 'masses' with whom Dr. Goebbels was
to operate. . . .

"Inflation is a tragedy that makes a whole people cynical,
hardhearted and indifferent. Having been robbed, the Germans became a nation of robbers."

The American economy has acquired an unmistakable inflationary propensity. The evidence can be found not only in the
pulsating upward movement of prices but also in dozens of
subtler phenomena.

In 1965, about 20% of the currency in circulation was in the
form of hundred-dollar bills. By 1980, that proportion had
doubled to 40% and merchants were buying cash registers with
an extra compartment to accommodate them. Before 1982, the
insurance industry defined a "catastrophe" as a disaster—a fire
or a flood—that caused more than a million dollars in damage.
Now the industry has inflated that definition to $5 million. In-
surance salesmen must sell $2.1 million in insurance policies to
qualify for the industry's million-dollar roundtable.

Most of the familiar symptoms of inflation-ridden societies
are already evident in the United States, at least in their rudi-
mentary forms. The national mood is inflationary. There is a
chilling similarity between the excesses of punk rock and the
desperate revelries of Brecht's Berlin. Inflation means there is
no tomorrow, no continuity, no moral or economic reckoning.
People learn to live without a sense of consequence.

The future becomes so confused and uncertain, so elementally unpredictable, that people camp in the present. In 1963,
economist F. A. Hayek once showed an English penny minted
a hundred years earlier to his Austrian students. They could
scarcely believe they were holding a coin that had maintained
its value for a century. A whole generation of young Ameri-

cans, those who have matured since the sixties, know money as something that dissolves unspent. They are the first American generation to hear talk of trillions. It is often called the "now" generation.

Every inflation brings a frenzied search for economic shelter in which nearly everyone involuntarily participates. Normally conservative men and women must gamble to stay even. In time, inflation becomes the central fact of economic and social life. In Buenos Aires, where the inflation rate was 450% in 1976 and 120% in 1982, crowds stand outside bank windows and punch pocket calculators as new exchange rates are posted. In Vienna, in the wild inflation of the early twenties, many of the famous coffee houses were driven from the best corners by banking offices.

Furious trading tends to drive out conventional productive activity. Inflation always spawns a breed of economic carpetbaggers who seek to profit from the gathering calamity and who spend their winnings in tasteless and conspicuous ways.

There is a lurching flight from currency into precious metals, diamonds, and paintings, which quickens as the rate of inflation increases and recedes when the rate recedes.

There is, typically, an increase in barter and illegal "off-the-books" transactions. The underground economy flourishes as barter becomes a national pastime.

While there has never been an inflation that was self-generating in the sense that prices continued to rise without increases in the money supply, many have become self-accelerating in the political sense that the pressures for still more inflation build as the problem worsens. This seems to explain the baffling persistence of nation after nation in a course that in retrospect is seen to be clearly disastrous. At any given point, though the prospect of even more inflation seems appalling, the prospect of stabilization appears to be just a little worse.

And of course large holders of precious metals, owners of houses with vastly inflated prices, commodity dealers, and publishers of gold-bug newsletters have a vested interest in the continuation of inflation.

The merger wave of the early eighties was evidence that a great many businessmen were expecting inflation to accelerate. And their expectation contributes to that acceleration. Speculators buy companies with money borrowed at high interest and count on inflation to reduce the real cost. They have invested in inflation and would be ruined by stability. Professor Peter Drucker reminds us that, publicly, the German industrialists "were, of course, for stable money and railed against that spendthrift government. But they had all invested in inflation and were committed to perpetuating it."

It was essential to the success of the hopeful therapies of the supply side that tax cuts would pressure politicians to cut spending. Milton Friedman said it plainly: "If the tax cut threatens bigger deficits, the political appeal of balancing the budget is harnessed to reducing government spending rather than to raising taxes."

But, in practice, the strategy led instead to a rationalization of deficit spending. Thus, we see 1980s American businessmen, like their counterparts in Weimar Germany, petitioning their president to cut taxes, in spite of the prospect of huge deficits. For, in a sickening economy, it is a sad commonplace that practically everyone seems to prefer inflation to taxes. A florist in North Carolina told his congressman, "We'd rather have big deficits if it means a cut in taxes. At least someone would have money in his pocket." A chorus of "amens" filled the room, according to *The New York Times*. In 1981, a major American brokerage firm advised its clients, "inflation can mean an increase in business activity and in actual production and profits and employment. . . ."

And in Danbury, Connecticut, a savings and loan officer told *The New York Times,* "High interest rates are forcing us to close up. At least inflation never made us close our doors."

The American economy may have a very limited tolerance for inflation. In primitive societies that function with little or no money—a nation of subsistence farms, for example—there is an immunity to inflation. Complexity and interdependence make a society more vulnerable.

By the spring of 1983, an administration that only two years before had pledged to eliminate deficits began to call its own projected record deficits ($208 billion for 1983) "structural," meaning presumably that deficits had become intrinsic, something beyond human control.

The Federal Reserve, as it had so often done before, spoke gravely about the need for restraint as the money supply broke out of its "target ranges" and continued its upward surge. The 1982 target range for M-1, the most basic measure of money supply, was 2½–5½%, or an average of 4%. By January 1983, M-1 was increasing at an annual rate of nearly 10%. M-2, a somewhat broader measure targeted for 6%–9%. was increasing, perhaps in part for "technical" reasons, at an annual rate of nearly 30% as the year turned.

Still, we tend to reject the inflationary reality: the public mood swings between hysteria when the price level is moving strongly upward and complacency when the rate of increase decelerates.

Persistent inflation is above all evidence that American society is in deep trouble. The Swiss scholar Wilhelm Röpke wrote, "Inflation, and the spirit which nourishes it and accepts it, is merely the monetary aspect of the general decay of law and of respect for law. . . . What is firm, durable, earned, secured and designed for continuity gives place to what is fragile, fugitive, fleeting, unsure and ephemeral. And that is not the kind of foundation on which the free society can long remain standing."

10

The Unmanageable State

"If it doesn't get any harder than that . . . it's a breeze."
Ronald Reagan, upon signing some papers
immediately after his inauguration

The ambivalence produced by the lack of any serious alternative to government action has disarmed the political establishment. The public wants the government to do more and cost less. Voters want, as Ronald Reagan perceived, to cut the cost of government in general without cutting anything in particular. Policy initiatives that satisfy—or seem to satisfy—these two conflicting imperatives are few and familiar.

There is the perennial proposal of whichever party happens to be out of power to make government more efficient—to get better results for less money—when it returns to office.

Jimmy Carter made this a centerpiece of his presidential campaign. If Roosevelt ran as a magician, Carter ran as an engineer. He saw in government a mechanism with almost unlimited money and power and the know-how to put a man on the moon. Why, he wondered, couldn't it make the trains run on time? We needed, he seemed to be saying, to get organized. "The mechanism of our government," he said, "should be made understandable, efficient, and economical." Then Mr. Carter ticked off the agenda, as if reading from a clipboard. He seemed annoyed that reforms so obvious to an engineer had been so long overlooked: "a drastic and thorough revision of the federal bureaucracy . . . tight, businesslike management techniques . . . abolish and consolidate . . . evolve clearly defined goals . . . an effective system of zero-based budgeting . . .

tough performance auditing ... efficient delivery systems."
But Carter was trying to rearrange a whirlwind.

It soon became evident that government would continue to
get bigger and less effective and there was very little Carter or
any president could do about it. W. Bowman Cutter, the top
OMB official in the Carter administration, later told *The Wall
Street Journal*, "an awful lot of people agree that the government is full of waste, but there isn't anything in the budget
that isn't like putting yourself in front of a locomotive if you
try to stop it." Thereafter, Mr. Carter seemed to wear a permanent stunned expression, as if elementally puzzled that
"our" government could not be made to work as well as his
watch. It was not that he had no power; his power was awesome. But the utility of power in complex human enterprises is
strangely limited.

It usually takes a year or so for a new administration to come
to the surprising realization that an American president's principal power—in domestic affairs—is the power to take blame,
and that his power to manage the federal establishment is
largely an illusion. "Power?" asked Lyndon Johnson. "The
only power I have is nuclear and I can't use that."

On February 26, 1970, Richard Nixon, as head of what was
then the strongest nation in the world, set out to abolish a single federal agency. "Too often in the past," he said, " 'sacred
cows' that have outlived their usefulness ... have been perpetuated because of the influence of small interest groups." He
announced his resolve to exterminate not anything as formidable as the Federal Trade Commission or the Small Business
Administration but only the seventy-three-year-old "Board of
Tea Tasters." (Later it turned out he had the name wrong; he
had meant the Board of Tea Experts, established by the Tea
Importation Act of 1897.) Less than three months later he had
backed down. His secretary of Health, Education and Welfare
reappointed the Board of Tea Experts and restored its money.

Roosevelt, with a vastly smaller bureaucracy, compared efforts to rouse or reform it to "pushing a feather bed." Harry

Truman said it was like pushing a wet noodle. Admiral Hyman G. Rickover, at a lower level, compared trying to make things work in government to sewing a button on a custard pie.

But such efforts are commonplace. Every administration in memory has sought to make government work better by managing it more systematically, by eliminating waste and fraud, by reducing paperwork. Like a feckless adolescent, government is forever auditing and reorganizing itself, making lists and tearful resolutions to get it together.

President Truman appointed the first Hoover Commission. Eisenhower appointed the second. Nixon appointed the Ash Commission. All three did work that was thorough and intelligent; all three made sensible specific recommendations, most of which were adopted. But the government did not get smaller and better. It got bigger and clumsier.

In 1980, the Advisory Committee on Intergovernmental Relations completed a multivolume study of the federal system. Its summary report said flatly, "Neither public officials nor the general public comprehend fully the new complexities of domestic public policy or adequately control—or even check—the myriad forces that have generated it." And later, "The system has become highly incomprehensible even to those whose job it is to have an overall understanding of it."

Efforts to impose discipline on the bureaucracy from the outside are as old as the Republic. Civil service, now more than a hundred years old, had a compelling rationale: to build a corps of professional public servants, chosen and promoted on merit, and to insulate them from patronage politics. Now civil service has become a device to nurture incompetence by insulating it from accountability. A century of civil service has made us long for the patronage system.

There have been, over the years, dozens of these cures for bureaucratic ineptitude. They all work perfectly well on paper. They have all been disappointing in practice.

The federal hiring freeze is a familiar device. Ronald Reagan said in his acceptance speech, "It is time our government should go on a diet. Therefore, my first act as Chief Executive will be to impose an immediate and thorough freeze on federal hiring." When in time he imposed one, he found that a freeze was already in force—Carter's third. Nixon had imposed two.

In the 1930s, the French built the Maginot Line—an unbreachable wall of firepower along the German border. It would make France forever immune to invasion from the north. It worked perfectly in theory. In the sterner weather of reality, however, the German generals acknowledged that the Maginot Line was impenetrable and went around it.

A hiring freeze is a nuisance, and agencies have found ways to circumvent it—by hiring "consultants," by increasing overtime, or by using temporary or part-time employees. And, if the ultimate intent is to contain the cost of government, its failure is manifest.

Whistle-blowing, a plan that encouraged bureaucrats to report instances of extravagance, is a particularly pathetic effort to curb federal extravagance. Ernest Fitzgerald, probably the most famous whistle-blower of all time, revealed a $2-billion overrun on a single weapons system, the C-5-A. Before his testimony, he'd been honored as the best weapons analyst in the Air Force. After his testimony, according to Senator William Proxmire, he was assigned to analyze a twenty-lane bowling alley in Thailand.

In response, President Carter installed a program to protect whistle-blowers from reprisals. But, in 1981, a study by the United States Merit Protection Board showed that nearly three-fourths of the employees who had witnessed waste and fraud had chosen not to report it because they believed nothing would or could be done about it. Only a fifth said they had kept quiet from fear of reprisal.

"Sunset laws" were designed to deal with the tendency of government programs to survive the disappearance of the problems they were established to solve. Colorado was the first to pass a sunset law, which obliges state agencies to rejustify their existence from time to time or expire. A number of other states passed similar laws.

In its first year, Colorado reviewed and eliminated three

agencies: the State Athletic Commission, established to regulate boxing (which did not exist in Colorado), the Board of Registration for Sanitarians, and the Board of Shorthand Reporters. The savings totaled $6810, but the review cost $212,000.

"Zero-based" budgeting, one of Mr. Carter's favorites, was a nostrum for the bureaucracy's tendency to get bigger every year rather than better. But its utility proved only rhetorical.

Such enterprises seem doomed. They can sometimes document the deficiencies of government, but they cannot correct them. Monopolistic enterprises are *inherently* inefficient. That cannot be changed. The most that auditors and efficiency experts can accomplish is the containment of the full effects of a chronic, incurable tendency.

There is a parallel effort to find some procrustean way to limit the growth of government—or at least to lock the balance between the public sector's requirements and the private sector's ability to pay before it is too late.

For twenty years, every administration has sought, or said it sought, to reduce the relative role of government. Some have even claimed to have done it. After two years in office, President Kennedy spoke of a decline in "federal expenditures in relation to population." In fact, the ratio had increased.

In his 1965 budget message, President Johnson predicted that "the ratio of federal spending to our total output will continue [sic] to decline." But between 1960 and 1968, the GNP increased 72%, defense spending increased 76%, and nondefense spending increased 134%.

Nixon raged that we should get the government off our backs and out of our pockets. But, in spite of the impression that he was starving public services, government grew faster, both absolutely and relatively, than in the Kennedy-Johnson years. Gerald Ford's Republican administration produced what was, until Reagan took office, history's biggest peacetime deficit.

Jimmy Carter was presented to the people as the arch enemy of big government. His handlers billed him as a crusading outsider who would "turn bloated government inside out." "Red ink," his treasury secretary told a group of businessmen, "makes this president see red."

In March 1978, after a year in office, Carter saw a huge deficit looming for 1980 and resolved to contain it. But, in fact, 1980 spending reached $579 billion and the deficit $59 billion—twice the limit Carter had set. "Federal spending," W. Bowman Cutter said flatly soon after Carter left office, "is out of control."

In less than two years, Ronald Reagan set three records: the biggest tax cut in American history, its biggest tax increase, and its biggest deficit.

The history of efforts to bring government under control is not encouraging. Government seems endlessly ingenious in evading the intent of measures to limit its growth. On March 17, 1971, Congress set a "permanent" limit of $400 billion on the amount of debt the federal government could incur. But now Congress agrees to increase the debt limit as routinely as it agrees to adjourn. Congress has since voted for twenty-three "temporary" increases. The "permanent" debt limit is still $400 billion; the "temporary" limit, in late 1982, $890.2 billion, for a total of $1.29 trillion.

There is a whole working science of circumvention. Costs can be hidden in dozens of different ways. The federal off-budget budget increased from $100 million in 1973 to $23.2 billion in 1981. At the state level, Pennsylvania has more than 2500 "OBEs," off-budget enterprises. Beyond off-budgeting is another new form, the government-sponsored agency, what Washington wits call off-off-budget entities.

In 1974, Congress passed the Federal Budget Act and brought into being a system designed to enable Congress to "get spending under control." The Act established new Budget Committees in both the House and Senate, and a Congressional Budget Office. The federal fiscal year was moved to September 30 to make way for two budget reviews, the first in the spring and the second in the fall. The first establishes targets for total spending and total revenues; the second makes these totals "binding." The logic of the Act was seductive. The new procedure gave Congress a way to see the budget whole, and to control it as a whole and not as an accidental aggregate of dozens of separate appropriations.

But the combined deficit for the three years after the Budget Act was three times that of the three years before the Act was passed. The process became, in practice, a way to rationalize deficits rather than to prevent them. It did not bring the budget process under control; it regularized the budget's upward momentum.

We have taken comfort in the assumption that the "independence" of the Federal Reserve system constitutes a check on the state's inflationary propensity, and it is part of the Potomac mythology that the Board is somehow insulated from politics. It is true that the Federal Reserve Board could, technically, stop inflation at any time. A Federal Reserve Board governor recently told the press, "My God, we all know what should be done in terms of restricting credit and balancing the budget." But, in practice, the Federal Reserve System, which employs 400 PhDs in economics in its Washington headquarters, has been the major instrument of inflation, the fabricator of the money that fuels inflation. Arthur Burns put it plainly in his splendid Per Jacobsson Lecture in Belgrade in 1979: "The Federal Reserve System had the power to abort this inflation. . . . It did not do so because the Federal Reserve was itself caught up in the philosophic and political currents that were transforming American life and culture." To fail to accommodate government's demand for money, however inflationary, he says later, "would be frustrating the will of Congress to which it was responsible." The Senate minority leader said recently, "It's time for Congress to wrest control of monetary policy from the hands of a tiny minority of monetary ideologues in the White House and the Federal Reserve."

As the old protections against the growth of the state have one by one been discredited, there has been a rush to design

new ones. In recent years, the public discourse has shifted
away from substance to the consideration of various proposals
to limit the power of government to tax or spend or both.
There is less and less debate about festering domestic problems—historic rates of unemployment among young people or
terror in the streets. Public policy is no longer much concerned
with how to solve problems, but how to contain or reapportion
the mounting costs of failure. A Democratic congressman said,
"There's no time for anything else and no interest in anything
else."

These proposals are little more than gimmicks, simplistic
and naive—not unlike the continuing quest for a diet that will
work in time for the prom and does not involve eating less. Just
as there has been a Mayo diet, an Air Force (or Drinking
Man's) diet, a Scarsdale diet, and an Atkins diet, there has been
a procession of proposals that promise to curb government
growth without confronting its cause. In my youth, there was
something called the Liberty Amendment, a constitutional
amendment that would have required the federal government
to auction the assets of its "enterprises" and use the proceeds
to retire or reduce the national debt. Since then there have
been a number of others—a flat (or at least flatter) and simpli-
fied income tax, a proposal to limit federal spending to a fixed
percentage of the GNP, proposals to oblige the federal government to balance its budget, proposals to restore the gold standard. . . .

These proposals are the political snake oil of the eighties—
efforts to repress the inevitable consequences of an urgent,
elemental, and unaltered appetite. They ask us to believe that
we can depoliticize politics by political action—rig democracy
so it will be immune to the traditional excesses of democracy.
The Heritage Foundation made an apparently serious proposal
to link congressmen's pay to their success in balancing the
budget on a sliding scale that would move from what was
$60,000 a year (it has since been raised to $69,762) to $500,000
if the deficit were eliminated.

As economist Rudolph Penner said, "it is difficult to make something·workable in the written Constitution if it's not in the unwritten Constitution. The people may favor a balanced budget in the abstract, but they think other things are more important."

The mentality that supports these nostrums, closer in spirit to fetishism than to responsible policy formation, is the same one that looks to price controls to control inflation and gun control to control crime, and, in the twenties, thought prohibition would eliminate drunkenness. In 1919, Congress passed the Volstead Act, criminalizing the sale of most alcoholic beverages. Evangelist Billy Sunday was ecstatic. "The reign of tears is over," he said. "The slums will be only a memory. We will turn our prisons into factories and our jails into corncribs. Hell will be forever for rent." Four years later, the population of federal prisons had doubled and per capita consumption of alcohol had increased. Similarly, revolutionary France failed to suppress its inflation even with price controls that called for death penalties for violators.

The proposed fiscal prohibitions all represent some sound principle. Government should not habitually monetize debt; government should not tax destructively; government should not grow so large as to crowd out the possibility of collective action outside government.

But these proposals are not cures; they are tardy preventatives masquerading as cures. They may become practical after we have solved the problem, after the role of government has been reduced to a manageable dimension. The enactment of such reforms could someday be one result of restoring institutional balance, but they could not bring that restoration about.

Caps of whatever kind, put in place before the source of the fiscal pressure is confronted and relieved, will simply put new pressure on a system that is already showing serious signs of strain. Nixon's price controls, following the classic pattern, repressed prices temporarily and then caused them to spurt and surge.

Repressive proposals will become a useful agenda if some institutional balance is restored. Money should someday be depoliticized. The banking system should be truly independent of government. There should, as Professor Hayek has proposed, be choice in currency. The power to force the acceptance of worthless paper as "legal tender" is an excessive power, too easily abused.

But these debates are premature. Such constraints made sense before Americans came to depend on government for essentials it cannot deliver. They may make sense again when these elemental dependencies have been corrected. But now it is both too late and too soon for them. Or, to reverse one of Lord Keynes' aphorisms, we cannot get thin by buying a smaller belt.

As President Reagan endorsed the balanced budget amendment in a ceremony in the Rose Garden, the National Council of Senior Citizens denounced it (correctly) as a "sneak attack on social security."

Philip Gramm, a Democratic congressman from Texas, writes about the disproportionate political power of federal beneficiaries. When he voted against a pay increase for federal employees, he received a thousand angry letters. "The largest National Association of Retired Federal Employees chapter in my district canceled a speech I was to give three days before the general election. They put my name in their national newsletters as one of their enemies." When he surveyed his constituents, he found that not one person in 10,000 who was not a federal employee knew how he had voted.

Senator William Proxmire receives a thousand letters a day. Only two or three of them, he says, support his crusade for economy. More than half (54%) the delegates to the Democratic Convention in 1980 were found to be on some government payroll. Paul Johnson, former editor of Britain's *New Statesman*, outlines the rough dimensions of America's welfare industry—5 million public and private welfare workers, distributing government payments and services to 50 million people.

Government, with the uneasy consent of the governed, is out of control. Richard Bolling, Democratic chairman of the House Ways and Means Committee, told a group of reporters, "Nothing has worked. Our policies are blowing up. We're factionalizing. We're unable to address obvious dilemmas ... something dreadful is going to happen unless we change."

There is a mounting concern that American democracy may be moving toward its final comeuppance, as observers have predicted it would since the beginning of the American experiment. Tocqueville saw some splendid values in American democracy but wondered about its stability. In the chapter of *Democracy in America* ominously titled "What Sort of Despotism Democratic Nations Have to Fear," he imagined a democratic form of despotism, a form "more extensive and more mild," that would "degrade men without tormenting them." "Democracy has a very bad track record," Lord Hailsham, presiding officer of England's House of Lords, said recently.

Half the federal budget is now spent for benefits to individuals, and two-thirds of these benefits are not linked to financial need. This is certain evidence of what historian Douglas North calls "the breakdown of the Madisonian political structure" built into the American Constitution in 1787 to prevent the political redistribution of wealth. Millions upon millions of people, rich and poor, have grown to depend on the state, and now, increasingly, their "entitlements" will be in conflict. Economic crisis may be only the prelude to a grave and irreversible political crisis.

In July of 1982, President Reagan stood on the steps of the Capitol with the Marine band playing in the background and urged Congress to approve a constitutional amendment that would require a balanced budget. A few weeks before, he had submitted to Congress a budget which the Congressional Budget Office figured would produce a $188 billion deficit.

And, at the same time, his party was running on national

television a paid advertisement featuring a postman from hometown America. "I'm probably one of the most popular people in town," he says. "I'm delivering social security checks with the 7.4 percent cost-of-living raise that President Reagan promised. He promised that raise and he kept that promise. In spite of the sticks-in-the-mud who tried to keep him from doing what we elected him to do."

11

The Gods That Failed:
The Limits of
Economics and Politics

"To know economics only is to know not even that."
—Wilhelm Röpke
(with apologies to Lichtenberg)

In the years following the New Deal, we came more and more to rely on economics to analyze our ills and on politics to set them right. The number of economists (Roosevelt called them "scientific economists") multiplied sixfold in that time, an increase curiously similar to the progress of inflation.

As government extended its near-monopoly of the public business, political action became overwhelmingly the principal instrument of change. As the distinction between society and state continued to blur, social action and political action became nearly identical.

The first activist economist attached to the New Deal White House, Lauchlin Currie, was an academic outcast, Harvard having denied him a permanent appointment. But overnight, economists who knew "how the Keynesian model can best be translated into policy" were in great demand in Washington.

In the bright Keynesian dawn, there seemed no limit to professional hubris. After the war, it was seriously proposed that an elite staff of economists in the Budget Bureau be empowered to control all taxing and spending so full employment could be maintained.

There was friction at first between the economists, newly set free from the cloister, and their cigar-chewing political partners. Edwin G. Nourse, a former president of the American Economics Association, was the first chairman of the Council of Economic Advisors. He saw the council as a "scientific agency" that would "bring the best available methods of social science to the service of the Chief Executive and of the Congress." But the subordination of science to politics began immediately. According to Charles Murphy, legal counsel in Truman's White House, "we found out that if it got late enough, Dr. Nourse would agree to anything. So we'd do most of the work after midnight."

For decades, economics was almost a priesthood. But by 1980, a White House economist told *The Wall Street Journal,* "Jokes about economists are replacing Polish jokes." President Carter said he knew a Georgia fortune teller who was a better forecaster than the White House economists.

Speaking on the fiftieth anniversary of the Great Crash, Marshall A. Robinson, president of the Russell Sage Foundation, said, "The economics profession, in sharp contrast to its position ten years ago, is divided and unsure . . . it speaks its prescriptions in muted voice and many tongues. It knows neither what ails the economy nor what should be done about it."

Partly, the trouble was specific. History had overtaken macroeconomics. Hayek spoke of a lost generation of economists who knew Keynesian economics and nothing else. The reconstruction of Nobel Prize–winning Keynesian James Tobin was typical. In December 1971, in his presidential address to the American Economic Association, he said, "Inflation lets this struggle [for conflicting claims on the nation's output] proceed, and blindly, impartially and non-politically scales down all its outcomes. There are worse methods of resolving group rivalries and social conflict." Seven years later, he had changed his mind. "Speaking for myself . . . I had been overoptimistic about the trade-off [between inflation and unemployment] and too skeptical of acceleration warnings." Leonard Silk wrote in

the summer of 1982 in *The New York Times*, ". . . the Keynesians regard the supply-siders as discredited, the supply-siders
regard the monetarists as discredited, and both the supply-
siders and monetarists regard Keynesianism as discredited."

But the disaffection with economics goes deeper. The 1981
annual meetings of the nation's economists became a remarkable collective lamentation over the state of the discipline.
Professor Mark Perlman of the University of Pittsburgh set the
tone. "Real doubt," he said, "has seized our profession." Professor Jack Barbash of the University of Wisconsin complained
that because rigor had become more important than substance, economic theory could be "nonsense in real-world
terms." Professor John Culbertson, also of the University of
Wisconsin, was most troubled of all. "Economics," he said, is
"failing to such an extent that the failure of economics may
play a central role in the failure of existing societies, even a serious crash in human civilization."

The Swedish economist Knut Wicksell had pointed out forty
years before *The General Theory* was published that economists habitually behaved as if they were advisers to benevolent
despots.

Keynes was captive of what his adoring biographer, Roy
Harrod, called the "presuppositions of Harvey Road," where
his family's Cambridge town house stood—the belief that
England would always be governed by a clubbish intellectual
aristocracy—England's best and brightest. Keynes hoped,
wrote a Harvard disciple, "that his economic ideas could be
put into practice outside the arena of partisan politics," and in
the introduction to the German edition of *The General Theory*,
Keynes says flatly that its prescriptions are "much more easily
adapted to the conditions of a totalitarian state."

Harrod wonders aloud whether Keynesian economics can
safely be mixed with democratic politics—whether "the small
group of intelligent people" could stay in control—whether
democratic government might "tend to get out of control and
act in a way in which the intelligent would not approve." He

concludes charitably that Keynes, enslaved to the presuppositions of Harvey Road, "did not give this dilemma the full consideration it deserves."

Harvard's Joseph Schumpeter, who knew Keynes and called him the most unpolitical of men, said, "the political game . . . interested him no more than did racing." And Virginia Woolf, recording in her diary a conversation with Keynes in the summer of 1918, notes his disillusion, his feeling that the governing classes were doomed, how at Versailles "men played shamelessly, not for Europe or even for England, but for their own return to Parliament at the next election."

Keynes had doubts of his own. In a letter to George Bernard Shaw in 1935, he wondered what "the final upshot of his work" would be after his new theory had been "duly assimilated and mixed with politics and feelings and passions." Toward the end of *The General Theory*, he repeated that uneasy question, wondering whether his ideas were properly rooted "in the motives which govern the evolution of political society"—whether "the interests which they will thwart [will be] stronger . . . than those which they will serve."

In that rare moment of doubt, when he seemed to question the presuppositions of Harvey Road, Keynes may have been at his most prophetic. For today the issue is not whether economic growth can be turned on and off at will by manipulating demand. We have largely discarded that idea as the destructive consequences of its application have become apparent. The question now is whether Keynes unwittingly popularized an approach to policy that destroys social equilibrium by so greatly reinforcing the tendency to centralize. Keynes is perhaps best remembered as the man who said, "In the long run we are all dead." Now it seems that Keynesian policies have put the political process at war with the public interest by helping to create a world in which what it takes to win elections in the short run results in an inflation-ridden, intolerable long run.

In the years after the death of Keynes, economics wandered

far beyond its natural limits. In the forties, in a kind of Faustian bargain, it traded its objectivity for power and influence. Beginning as the central instrument of national domestic policy, economics soon became in practice a rationalization for the growth of the state.

A researcher has estimated that by the mid-1970s, 40% to 50% of the profession consisted of full- or part-time government employees or recipients of government grants—what he calls the "insiders"—and that an equal number of "outsiders" were linked less formally to the central establishment. In other words, more than four-fifths of the men and women in the profession were directly or indirectly on the payroll of the state.

Today, economics has little left to contribute. The problems that trouble America can still be described in economic terms, but the cure is beyond its reach.

J. B. Burnham of Pittsburgh's Mellon Bank wrote in the fall of 1979, "The heyday of the economists as the authorities on inflation may be over. They have described, very effectively, the superstructure of the contemporary inflationary process. But mere description or understanding of intricate economic relationships is not enough." The cause of the present economic malaise is a *social* imbalance: the assumption by the state of large and essential responsibilities that it cannot exercise. And economics is powerless either to explain that imbalance or to correct it.

An even more elemental disenchantment has become unmistakable. After decades of believing that we could reshape society by the way we voted, the electorate has become disaffected—not merely with particular parties or politicians, but with the political process itself. In a nation obsessed by limits, those least explored have been the limits of politics. But now people are feeling betrayed by the process they were taught to believe was their salvation.

The most surprising and significant apostasy from the religion of politics was that of Theodore H. White. In the years since 1960, when he had launched his fabulously successful quadrennial chronicles of American politics, Teddy White had lost the faith. In the beginning, he had promised a book after each presidential election from 1960 to 1980. But he skipped 1976 altogether and wrote a personal memoir instead, and his 1980 book used a halfhearted description of the Carter-Reagan contest as a vehicle for a public renunciation of politics.

White believed for years that he was recording an historic adventure in the practice of democracy wherein the people's highest hopes—for a society that was just and caring, secure and responsible—were being made real.

"Somehow," he wrote, "public affairs had gone off the track. . . . Somewhere, in the decades of upheaval, came a wrong turning." What we had once called the Great Society had become "simply a place." There was a question "whether it could continue to be a nation." The man who had seemed determined for decades to think the best of politics and politicians was deeply disillusioned. On civil rights: "In trying to eradicate racism, the politics of the sixties and seventies has institutionalized it. . . ." On the cities: ". . . with all the attention and programs, big cities were on their way to tragedy." On the goals of liberalism: "They had set out to free everyone and had created a nation of dependents instead." On the federal budget: ". . . no one, absolutely no one, can control the budget of the United States—not the President, not the OMB, not Congress."

White had at last begun to wonder whether politics could repair the damage politics had wrought, whether we had come to "an end to a system of politics that had outlived its time." On a bored, restless day a few weeks before the election, White wrote in his journal, "How long can you stay interested in inflation and the tax cut? There were five national elections in Germany the year before Hitler came to power in 1933: the last, which Hitler won, showed a sharp drop-off in votes. We've had politics up to our ears. . . ."

This kind of disillusioned foreboding is becoming general. In

1981, a study commissioned by the Connecticut Mutual Life Insurance Company found that political disaffection had become epidemic. More than half the people surveyed said they do not believe important national problems—inflation, energy shortages, crime—can be solved through political action. (Half do not believe the way they vote determines how the country is run.)

Political participation has been declining for nearly a quarter of a century—roughly since the beginning of the Great Inflation. The easy assumption has been that those who don't vote don't care or are so "present-oriented," to borrow Professor Edward Banfield's term, that they are uninterested in activities that are unlikely to affect their lives before nightfall. To some unknowable extent this is certainly true.

But opinion researchers are beginning to find another meaning in these mounting abstentions. A week before the 1980 election, for example, California pollster Merv Field told the press, "The public is increasingly coming to the dismaying and fearful realization that inflation, as well as more of the other substantive issues, are beyond the ability of the President to do much about." Voters saw the election, Field said, "as a grade-10 Hobson's Choice."

The two-party system is showing signs of strain, but opinion analyst Everett Ladd, director of the Roper Center for Public Opinion Research at the University of Connecticut, a careful student of political trends, sees not a realignment in progress but a *de*alignment. He writes of the "growing incapacity of the political parties to organize the electorate." In 1952, 22% of the Americans of voting age called themselves "Independent." By 1980, the percentage had increased to 40%. "Since people are of mixed minds about what the government should be doing," Ladd writes in *Public Opinion,* "they naturally are tied only lightly to the contending parties and to their murky blueprints for the future." About half the registered members of both major political parties could see no important differences between the parties. *The New York Times'* Adam Clymer called the 1982 election results "a measure of the public's lack of conviction that any of the political alternatives offered it are really adequate."

It was no wonder. The parties have little left to say. The Democrats seemed privately relieved to have lost power and responsibility in 1980. Now, in 1983, the Republicans have nothing left but a failed program. The Democrats are frankly rummaging among old platforms and position papers for some alternative. It was as Tocqueville wrote of French politics: "The parties themselves, decimated, apathetic and weary, longed to rest for a time during a dictatorship of any kind, provided only that it was exercised by an outsider and that it weighed upon their rivals as much as on themselves. . . . When great political parties . . . reach the point of wishing less to succeed than to prevent the success of their opponents, one should prepare for servitude—the master is near."

Political indifference is a common accompaniment to chronic inflation. Professor Harry Johnson, who knows inflationary societies well, writes that because inflation redistributes income from the broader mass of people to certain favored groups, "it is easy enough to build a traditional politics of left and right on divisions among a minority of beneficiaries from inflation, such that control of inflation is a political issue before elections, a pious promise after elections and an intentionally non-effective policy at all times." Politics, Johnson concludes, becomes a charade, and "the majority devotes itself to the more earnest business of earning a living in spite of inflation and the politics that perpetuates it."

Out at the edge of American society, surprising numbers of persons are beginning to look for protection or even escape from a society they believe may be coming to pieces. "For the first time in my life," one worried "survivalist" told *The Wall Street Journal*, "I'm beginning to think that our country could perish if we don't take the right steps." A couple in Gresham, Oregon, keeps five packed suitcases ready at the back door.

Grocers are buying bulletproof aprons. A supplier advertises "fashion-conscious ballistic apparel"; for $1200 you can buy a bulletproof umbrella "good for shielding submachine-gun fire." In California, housewives can sign up at Sears for courses in how to use Mace.

A number of bestsellers offer bizarre survival advice. Howard J. Ruff, in the most successful financial book of all time (it reportedly sold more than 3 million copies), advises retreat to a small town and stockpiling of food, light bulbs, motor oil, and laundry detergent. But there are factions in the survival movement, and many find Ruff's scenario for disaster far too tame. They advise a heavily fortified wilderness retreat for protection against "roving bands" presumably in search of scarce detergent. Another sneers at this advice. "Don't forget," he writes, "in any conceivable howling mob these days, you'd have to suppose the presence of highly trained experts such as vets of Special Forces, paratroop units and Marine Recon Units. . . . A far better strategy is . . ."

The childish, morbid imagination of the survivalists seems boundless. The Center for Survival Research in Mount Vernon, New York, sells books describing "America's Secret Survival Havens," the best places to live in the worst of times, three volumes for $39.95 chargeable to Visa or MasterCard, including as a bonus a detailed map of America's safest retreats.

But Karl Hess contends that one can withdraw from society without leaving suburbia. "The greatest security a man can know," he writes in a letter promoting his *Survival Tomorrow* newsletter, "is his ability to be self-sufficient." And he offers a checklist of "Things you can do to turn your suburban home into a secure 'survival retreat.' "

Dealers in the accessories of survival estimate that between 2 and 5 million Americans are regular or occasional customers for English Wildcat Quality Crossbows, water purifiers, bullet-making machines, and freeze-dried chicken and noodles at $19.50 a case.

It is the ultimate form of quackery. The pushers of this

equipment beg you, for your own sake, not to count the cost. "There is no such thing," one of them writes, "as 'not being able to afford' whatever course of action will best lead to your survival."

Scholars are finding that these idiocies represent the further reaches of a nearly universal state of mind. In almost identical surveys, twenty years apart, the more recent in 1976, the University of Michigan's Institute for Social Research confirmed that Americans were becoming more present-oriented, that their confidence in institutions was shattered and that their sense of community was decaying. America was becoming, as Theodore White feared, "just a place." People were turning to "more idiosyncratic solutions to the problems of living." Social psychologist Kenneth Keniston summarized the evidence: "The Sixties did not produce a determination to improve society through concerted collective action. On the contrary, most Americans have fallen back on that older American fantasy of the lone cowboy seeking personal fulfillment in an empty desert."

Economist Herbert Stein said the same thing in another way: "Books about the collapse of the economic system were as popular in the 1930s as they are in the 1980s. There is, however, a difference. The books of the 1930s were about how to construct a better system after the old one had collapsed. The books of the 1980s are about how the reader can make his fortune out of the collapse of the system."

No alternative social vision is available to the survivalists. The state is failing, and there seems to be no alternative to the state. Douglas Casey, author of the bestselling *Crisis Investing*, puts the matter with an almost perfect clarity. "If a service cannot be provided profitably," he writes bravely, "that is *de facto* evidence that it is not worth providing." For him there is nothing between the individual and the state but a vast no-man's land.

Both the political left and the political right are coming to separate dead ends for the same reason. The collapse of confidence in what we have relied on so exclusively for so long has left a dark and dangerous void. One of the wealthier survivalists wistfully said to a reporter that he'd take a dollar-a-year job if it offered a chance to "do something for mankind." The practices and beliefs that gave American society its cohesion are falling into disuse and disrepute, and we have nothing to put in their place. As the state grows larger, the stature of the men who lead it grows smaller. Into vacuums like these, historically, have entered the confidence men, the miracle workers, the men on horseback.

G. K. Chesterton said that when people stop believing in God, they do not begin to believe in nothing; they begin to believe in anything. There is a seller's market in political-economic snake oil. Half-mad, half-informed, magic cures become the basis of serious national debate. Journalist Jude Wanniski called the early members of his supply-side cabal "the wild men."

A splintering of American politics is evident in its exploding lexicon. For years there were only conservatives and liberals. Now there are neoconservatives, neoliberals, new rightists, new leftists, libertarians in several shades and, most recently, MARs—middle American radicals. Political analyst Kevin Phillips sees us closer to the government-controlled capitalism of the corporate state than we were in the thirties. He reminds us that, in times of turmoil, Americans searching for normalcy turn, traditionally, not to conservatives but to populist politicians from chainsaw country with names like "Pitchfork Ben," "Sockless Joe," and "The King Fish." Phillips imagines a coalition of big business and the new right offering something that might be called the "Economic Security State." This would require closer federal management of the economy to promote growth and to reindustrialize and restore our ability to compete in world markets. Heavy industry would be shored up in the interest of national defense, and the entitlements of farmers, wage earners, pensioners, and the middle class guaranteed. The recipe for this "apple pie authoritarianism" is an agenda strikingly similar at the core to that of the so-called new liberals. And Teddy White can only hope for a new generation of politicians who will somehow use their power to re-create community.

12

Where Do We Go from Here?

"... it is not enough [for those who write in the democratic age] to show what events have occurred. They wish to show that it could not have occurred otherwise. They take a nation arrived at a certain stage of its history and affirm that it could not but follow the track that brought it thither."

Alexis de Tocqueville

In the fifty years since the Great Depression, history has discredited the principal premises on which the modern welfare state was built. America has created a giant, monopolistic public service conglomerate by mistake, built on a series of interlocking misapprehensions.

It was Keynes' central premise, and later Roosevelt's, that the American economy had reached maturity, that there would henceforth be a chronic shortage of jobs and a chronic surplus of capital. But history has proved that premise and its corollaries dead wrong. Today it is clear that Keynes' work is most deficient in the quality he most wanted for it: the principal propositions of *The General Theory* are not general.

Joseph Schumpeter wrote in 1946, the year of Keynes' death, an appreciative but brutal summation of the mind and meaning of Keynes. The economist was, he said, "surprisingly insular." His advice, Schumpeter points out, was always English advice, yet Keynes "always exalted what was at any moment truth and wisdom for England into truth and wisdom for all times and places."

England's situation after World War I was unique. The country was broke. Its weakened social fabric, as Schumpeter said, had become rigid. Taxes and wages were too high to permit rapid reconstruction of the economy. Keynes believed that to return to the gold standard at pre-war parity would be suicidal. (Gold, he correctly told his friends, would soon be reduced to the status of a constitutional monarch.) And so he prescribed monetary management.

Keynes' model makes sense only if—and it is a towering "if"—the industrial plant remains static; if, as so many believed during the thirties, the economic point of no return has been reached. But industrial *change*, the creation of new plants built on new technologies—the phenomenon that has most distinguished twentieth-century capitalism—is a concept beyond the reach of the Keynesian model, with its assumption of stagnation.

Keynesian economics, as presented in *The General Theory* is, as Professor Hicks contends, the economics of an era of depression. It is an economics of special cases. Schumpeter writes: "Keynesians may hold that these special cases are the actual ones of our age. They cannot do more than that."

Today we know that what was taken for chronic stagnation was in fact temporary, that the economies of Europe and America were not mature, but barely adolescent. The Keynesian edifice, which posited this "maturity" before the air age, before the computer, before microwave transmission, before the laser, before space travel, before automation, before robotics, rested on a false foundation. In his magnum opus, Keynes had reasoned brilliantly from a false premise, much as he had so often done, merely for practice, on the worn square of carpet from which the Apostles read their papers to each other. Keynes and the Keynesians had mistaken the late dawn of the industrial era for its twilight. And, as a result, the potentially healthy American economy has been under intensive care for nearly fifty years.

The fragility which the American economy showed during the thirties was not, as was so widely assumed, a reflection of an inherent weakness, but a temporary condition induced by mistaken public policies. There is no solid consensus on what caused the Crash and delayed the recovery, but there is a near consensus on what did not. Whether the Great Depression was the result of a deliberate reduction of the money supply that asphixiated the economy, or was caused by the imposition of a mercantilistic tariff policy that suddenly shut off foreign markets when they were needed most, or some combination of these and other factors, is still being debated.

In the early thirties, the Federal Reserve allowed the money supply to contract by 30% over a period of several years. Economist Gottfried Haberler reminds us that today economists tremble when the money supply fails to increase by some targeted amount. During the Great Depression it *fell* nearly a third. Moreover, in 1932, the Hoover administration nearly doubled income taxes, increasing the top-bracket rate, for example, from 24% to 63%. And later, by raising bank reserve requirements, the Federal Reserve may have induced the steep slide of 1937.

To make matters worse, Congress passed the Smoot-Hawley tariff, history's highest, in 1931. A staggering number of economists for that time, 1028 altogether, vainly urged the president to veto the bill. In an open letter to *The New York Times*, they warned that stifling trade would never create employment. To some unknowable extent, Smoot-Hawley helped prolong the Great Depression.

There is an unmistakable tendency for economic activity to follow a cyclical course, to ebb and flow, and scholars are forever scrutinizing the evidence in search of patterns and chains of causation. But logic and experience suggest that, in the absence of central intervention, this rising and falling does not tend to be cumulative, but self-correcting. The Great Depression was clearly not a natural disaster but an artificial one.

Today we are able to question the cocksure conventional wisdom of the postwar period which says that World War II "cured" the Depression. It seems far more likely that Pearl Harbor merely suspended the prevailing prejudice against production. Temporarily freed from the fear that they were destroying their jobs, men and women began to produce wholeheartedly again.

Before the mobilization began, there had been an all-out effort to limit production, to plow crops under, to "spread the work," to push men and women out of the labor force. Overnight, that attitude was turned inside out as patriotism triumphed over economic superstition. Attempts to limit the work week gave way to efforts to extend it. Factories painted their windows black and worked around the clock. Retired persons rejoined the labor force by the tens of thousands. There was again, as there had been for decades, an acute labor shortage. Twenty million women went to work, many in jobs that had formerly been defined as off-limits for them. Teenagers were let out of school to harvest the crops. Factories proudly flew "E" flags awarded for high productivity.

And, when the war was over, in less than a year the economy adjusted to a *reduction* in the level of federal spending almost as large as the massive mobilization increases. The estimates of postwar unemployment had to be revised almost immediately. In December 1945, just as the House passed its version of the Employment Act, the *Times* reported that the official estimate of spring unemployment had been reduced from 8 million to 5 million. President Truman had to admit that unemployment was not "so serious or drastic" as his advisers had predicted.

Henry Wallace, in a popular postwar book, called for a continuation of wartime spending levels to put 54 million to work—a goal considered irresponsibly utopian. Twelve months after V-J day, employment was 57,050,000 *without* the therapies suggested by the Employment Act.

The reconversion provided astounding evidence of an economic vitality which so many had come to believe had been lost. First came the basics: fuel, clothing, and food. In the Southwest, oil, cotton, and cattle became the basis for a boom that is still going on.

There was a pent-up demand for familiar pre-war products—automobiles (by 1949, the industry finally exceeded 1929
production), radios, and refrigerators. There were also dozens
of new products.

The war ended on August 14. By November, the Edison
Electric Appliance Corporation, using methods learned during
the war, had converted from making armor-piercing bullet
cores to the manufacture of fully automatic dishwashers—at a
third less than pre-war prices. This was one example among
thousands.

(One automobile company found it would have been
cheaper all around had they locked up their automobile plant,
built another for war work, scrapped it when the war was
over, and moved back to the original plant to make cars again.)

This adjustment, which contradicted a practically unanimous pessimism, was accomplished during a massive reduction
of federal spending.

In fiscal 1945, which ended June 30, the federal government
spent more than $100 billion. The next year spending *fell* more
than a third to $65 billion. The decline was four times as much
as *total* federal spending just six years before.

By VJ-Day, the war was consuming almost half the gross national product. Between 1945 and 1946 the figure fell from
42% to 12%, and a year after that it fell to 8½%. Yet the belief
in the hazard of high productivity has persisted with awesome
tenacity. The fear that the supply of work may someday dwin-
dle and disappear still expresses itself in dozens of ways. Even
the generation born in the industrial age is not immune to it; it
seems to be in the blood.

Work rules continue to outlaw efficient methods and mandate obsolete ones. Workers rarely attack machines anymore,
but they cripple them by limiting their use or canceling their
advantages, as when standby musicians must be paid when recorded music is used in a Broadway theater. Without the Luddite rationalization, practices like these would be seen as simple extortion.

The economy still struggles against high productivity—even as American producers lose markets to foreign competition. Thus, the belief that an economy is prone to decline causes it to decline. There are men and women still living who can remember the days when employment opportunities seemed inexhaustible, when there was an abiding shortage of labor. The Old World exported its unemployment to the United States. The capacity of the American economy to put people to work was not feeble and tentative but surging and insatiable. We offered work to millions, many unskilled and illiterate. Unemployment, the existence of a pool of men and women who wanted work, was not seen as a social burden to be dealt with dutifully and sacrificially. Workers were scarce and sought after: the system wanted and welcomed them.

But the Great Depression, however mistakenly, changed all that. There was and is a tenacious fear of a chronic labor surplus. We began to ration work, to look for reasons to exclude people from it. And the impulse survives. Young people, for example, are still banned from the work force, often at the peak of their innocent audacity and enthusiasm. "Child labor" is perceived as the ultimate outrage, but the root of the antagonism to it was the fear that children would take jobs men needed to feed their families. It is not proposed that six-year-olds be obliged to work from dawn to dark in dangerous mines or satanic mills. But to exclude young people from the serious work of the world because of an exhausted supposition that there is not enough work to go around is grossly unfair to them.

The Luddite impulse persists, as the expectation of a labor surplus leads to policies that produce an apparent labor surplus. In 1982, it was proposed to relax the restrictions on fourteen- and fifteen-year-olds for the first time since the Great Depression. The new rules would have permitted these young people to work six more hours a week, when school is in session, to a total of twenty-four. It would have opened certain kinds of work now forbidden: the operation of switchboards, teletypewriters, and data processing equipment, filling orders in warehouses and polishing trucks and buses. The AFL-CIO protested. "At a time when their older brothers and sisters cannot find work," President Lane Kirkland told the press, "it is preposterous to lower the working rules for school-age youngsters."

In the same way and for the same reason, older people are arbitrarily shelved regardless of their preference. Bismarck chose sixty-five as the retirement age when he was setting up his social security system because so few people in that era lived that long. If, in the 1880's, it excluded people unnecessarily from the work force, the numbers were very small. But since then, life expectancy has nearly doubled—and millions of able-bodied older men and women spend decades in a retirement forced upon them by the folklore of chronic stagnation.

The social security system was conceived at a time of a presumably critical capital surplus. Thus, unlike private pension plans, its premiums were not invested. Beneficiaries were to be paid not from accumulated reserves but from the current contributions of the working population. This method, which pushed the cost of benefits forever forward to future generations was, curiously, called a pay-as-you-go system. Now social security is in desperate trouble and the pay-as-you-go financing method seems scandalously improvident. But the Depression mentality would have been incapable of selecting a method that would have added capital to an economy which seemed to be suffering from a severe and disabling abundance of capital. The idea of capital shortage was then scarcely imaginable.

These and other anomalies have contributed to a gathering recognition that not only was the accepted economic diagnosis of the Depression era mistaken, but also policies based on that diagnosis created the very conditions they were designed to remedy. The euthanasia of the rentier was premature and ill-advised.

Of all the conclusions drawn from the Depression experience, the ones least examined were not economic but social:

that independent institutions proved inherently incapable of dealing with the problems of the industrial era; that full employment and retirement security had to be provided by the central authority if they were to be provided at all.

There is no question that, after three years of Depression, these assumptions seemed sound. The independent sector did not in fact provide adequate stability and security during the grim years of 1929–1932. But that did not mean that it never could.

The modern welfare state is in a sense the product of a misunderstanding, compounded by some cruel accidents of timing. Wilhelm Röpke, the Swiss political-economist-philosopher who was the intellectual godfather of the post-World War II German economic "miracle," describes this central paradox of the modern era: *what we call the welfare state grew most rapidly after the need for it had largely disappeared.* The large-scale requirement for social assistance resulted from a highly specific, ephemeral circumstance. As industrialization progressed, the old pre-industrial patterns of mutual support disintegrated. The individual became a bewildered, dependent, isolated member of the new industrial proletariat, a refugee in his own society.

"The paradox," Röpke writes in *A Humane Economy* (published in English translation in 1960), "is that the modern welfare state carries to an excess the system of government-organized mass relief precisely at a moment [he was writing in the late 1950s] when the economically advanced countries have largely emerged from that transition period and when, therefore, the potentialities of voluntary self-help by the individual or group are greatly enhanced." Massive state intervention was merely an expedient, made necessary by a society that was changing radically but unevenly, whose economic institutions were adapting more slowly. We were suffering from an acute, though probably temporary, institutional lag.

The expedient of state assistance, Röpke writes, "was necessary as long as most factory workers were too poor to help themselves, too paralyzed by their proletarian position to be provident, and too disconnected from the old social fabric to rely on the solidarity and help of genuine small communities."

Today, the industrialized nations have advanced well beyond that stage, and "the welfare state has outlived its necessity . . . it derives its origin and meaning from the conditions of an all but finished transition period of economic and social development."

But what Röpke could see in the late fifties as a difficult transition was seen in the thirties as a possibly terminal illness. After three years of stagnation, the American economy was perceived as being permanently disabled. Most Americans did not see its independent institutions as experiencing an adjustment; they saw them in ruins. It was easy to believe that a maturing economy had produced problems that were beyond the reach of independent institutions.

Just as the economic diagnoses fulfilled themselves—the belief in stagnation producing stagnation and the belief in labor surplus producing labor surplus—the social diagnosis became self-fulfilling. The universal assumption that the independent sector could not adapt to the needs of an industrial society guaranteed that it would not make that adjustment. The state quickly monopolized the new agenda of public business and, in time, very nearly the whole of it. Thus, the independent sector was doomed by a limiting definition to perpetual adolescence. By the 1980s, American pluralism had almost disappeared and our society's perception of itself had become grossly distorted.

In every major period in the history of science, a certain model, or paradigm, of the universe has been widely accepted. This dominant paradigm provides an outline or framework of the workings of the physical world. Scientists work to fill in the details by observation and experimentation. Some of the facts they find fit the paradigm, or seem to; and others do not. Any divergence of fact—of reality—from the model creates a certain strain. When it becomes too great, a scientific revolution occurs. Scientists renounce the old paradigm and adopt a new one. The investigatory agenda is radically revised. For cen-

turies, for example, the Ptolemaic cosmology was the dominant scientific paradigm. In time, in a painful upheaval, it gave
way to the Copernican model.

Sheldon J. Wolin, in his splendid essay "Paradigms and Political Theories," has suggested that, in a similar way, social
decisions are shaped by a dominant social paradigm.

A society has a self-image, a set of widely shared beliefs
about how it sets goals and gets things done, about where its
strength resides, about its structure and the relationship of its
parts, about how responsibilities are defined and distributed.
In other words, Wolin says, a society "believes itself to be one
thing and not another."

As with scientific paradigms, there is an abiding tension between reality and the prevailing social paradigm. When the
divergence creates too great a strain, a conceptual revolution
occurs. People repudiate the old social paradigm and embrace
a new one. The new paradigm suggests a new way of looking
at and understanding the world, and provides a fresh blueprint
for social renovation.

Wolin has found throughout history an intimate relationship
between social crisis and innovative social theory. When societies begin to break down, when institutions begin to totter
and authority to decompose, a search begins for a new paradigm, a new and imaginative "representation of what society
would be like if it could be reordered." Constructive change
begins when people begin to imagine an alternative.

In the fifty years since the Great Crash, we have come to
accept a holistic corporatist social cosmology with an all-em-
bracing state at the center. Whatever happens is the business
of the state; if other institutions exist, they are subordinate to
the state. Institutions outside the state draw their legitimacy
from the state, must justify their existence to the state, exist at
the pleasure of the state. The state *is* the society. What is unofficial is illegitimate. Private education is called "divisive"; its
existence undermines the state. The idea of community is expressed only through the state.

What the state does "works" by definition. What the state

does not do does not fit the paradigm—is unreal, or less real. Thus, any reduction in the size of the state diminishes the public good.

As a black judge, A. Leon Higginbotham said at Yale in the spring of 1982, "Anything that talks about a dilution of federal involvement can be translated as a reduction of resources, particularly for the weak, the poor and black."

The intellectuals in National Socialist Germany believed that local governments were redundant because there was no longer any distinction between the people and the government. Leninists have contended for years that there is no need for independent trade unions because the Party is the embodiment of the working class.

When a Brooklyn family and their friends began to spend their Saturday mornings scrubbing a filthy Williamsburg subway station, they were ordered to desist. The head of the Transport Workers Union said that if the Transit Authority did not do the work officially, it should not be done.

But in this country and elsewhere, this monolithic, corporate social paradigm can no longer contain or explain social reality. People are beginning to realize that a large and growing fraction of social reality exists separately from the state, is beyond the reach of the state, is largely incomprehensible to the state and unresponsive to the only methods of coordination available to the state. There is a gathering awareness of how much work is done not because of the state but in spite of it, and hence how much of society's future will be shaped outside the state.

13

The Italian Solution

"Millions of individuals work, produce, and save, despite
everything we can invent to impede, stop or discourage them."
—Luigi Einaudi
former president of Italy

To some substantial but unknowable extent, societies everywhere are moving to protect themselves from incompetent
governments. This collective instinct for self-preservation is
proving to be a force of remarkable power. The economic aspect of the impulse has manifested itself in the worldwide formation of "second" or "alternative" economies. The dominant
social paradigm of the moment obliges us to view these other
economies as abnormal, irregular, or illegitimate, so they are
usually called "clandestine," "underground," or "subterranean." But now their sheer size is making them visible—our
own irregular economy may be as large as the regular economy of France—and civil disobedience becomes legitimate as
it becomes pandemic. These economies are healthy and growing rapidly. The official economies are, most of them, in decline.

In terms of the dominant social paradigm, the alternative
economies are inhabited by chiselers and tax dodgers. But they
can also be seen as unplanned, uncoordinated efforts to protect
societies from confused and destructive central authorities.
While the United States government was talking about con-
triving economic revival by exempting a few designated urban
"enterprise zones" from certain disabling taxes and regulations, a quarter of the economy had already exempted itself

from taxes and regulation and was growing three times faster than the "regular" economy. The flight to gold amounts to the natural selection of a sounder money for a softening one.

The state could conceivably in time become a useless façade, with no supporting substance. Political philosopher Michael Walser has written appealingly in his *Radical Principles* about "the hollowing out of the state." It has lately become possible to imagine—I do not wish to imply it is anywhere imminent—what might be called the shedding of the state. The elements are to be found in many modern societies: government services deteriorating so badly that they function barely or not at all; people evading or escaping the taxes that support services they perceive as useless; people devising alternative patterns of service in the vacuum created by the paralysis of the state. Thus could the underground society, the so-called subterranean society, in time become the dominant one, and the institutions of the official society, having been reduced to a rigid, useless shell, could simply be shed.

In Italy, this social metamorphosis, this process of spontaneous social transformation, is apparently farthest advanced. Many government employees, for example, simply hang their hats on the office hatrack to signify that they are technically "at work." But they are actually elsewhere, more often than not working in the "economia sommersa" (submerged economy). Rome's official post office, for example, has 1500 employees. A parallel private post office, "Romana Recapiti," delivers an equal amount of mail with 300 workers, most of whom are moonlighting employees of the official post office. Italians, it is said, are socialists in the morning and capitalists in the afternoon.

In fact, there are two Italies, increasingly distinct. Italy's official economy is dominated by the state holding companies—the first established by Mussolini in 1933—in steel, shipbuilding, communications, energy, and banking. These closely controlled enterprises, absurdly inefficient, are sustained by immense, inflationary "loans." They, along with the government bureaucracy, are highly politicized. Even the use of hospital operating rooms is allocated on the basis of the surgeons' political affiliation. Such official entities, which consume well over half of Italy's recorded GNP, form a vast patronage system. Everyone wants "il posto," a job in the official system (in China such a post is called an iron rice bowl), or at least to be designated an invalid, joining the 6 million Italians who receive a monthly check for some official but often imaginary disability.

But absenteeism is the rule and work the exception. Ministries, where the official hours are from eight to two, are places where employees arriving "a little late" meet on the stairs those who are leaving "a little early." One Palermo street cleaner, perhaps Italy's champion absentee, missed 1278 days of work in five years because of "hypochondria." Officially Italy is bankrupt, its huge monetized deficits producing chronic double-digit inflation.

But there is another Italy. "Faced with an untenable situation," writes the *International Herald Tribune,* "huge numbers of Italians have decided to ignore rather than try to change the system." Two-thirds of the Italian workers have a second job. Six million Italians work illegally. Half of Italy's officially "unemployed" workers have a steady job.

The full dimensions of this irregular Italy are unknown and unrecorded, so the official statistical picture of the Italian economy has little relation to reality. Naples is one of Italy's largest glovemaking centers, but, according to official statistics, no gloves are made in Naples.

Italy's Study Center for Social Investments says that large numbers of Italians, "sheltered from the law and remote from political power, are carving out for themselves little beachheads of illegality and sweetness of life." These little beachheads, taken together, are what make the nation work. Some say that half of Italy's GNP is produced by small, often illegal firms and by their first cousins, firms deliberately kept small to avoid the costly labyrinth of Italian labor law.

Prato, west of Florence, is the center of a booming textile industry, consisting of thousands and thousands of small enterprises. The small, low-cost steelmakers of Brescia, the Bresciani, have grown rapidly against the tide of a recession in big European steel. "Italy's weak and inefficient government can't hold in check the natural enterprise and imagination of the Italian people," writes Barbara Ellis in *Forbes* magazine.

The growth of such countereconomies is worldwide. They bear differing names. Italy's "economia sommersa" is called "the back door" in Communist China. The French call it "travail au noir"; the Germans "Schattenwirtschaft" (shadow economy)." In Russia, the economic underground is "the second economy"; Israel's is "Kalkala schora"; Britons call it "fiddling." Citizens of a Southeast Asian nation call their shadow economy Corporation 23 because all official economic activity is carried on by twenty-two state corporations.

Some economists estimate that in India the "black" economy may equal the "white," or legal economy. In 1981, the Indian government offered (unsuccessfully) special, no-questions-asked, high-yield bonds to lure some of the "black" money back into the "white" world.

Britain's irregular economy is estimated to be 15% of the GNP, having doubled in the last ten years, as law-abiding Britons have found it morally acceptable; 59% of the British still think fox hunting is morally wrong, but only about half that many, 31%, think it is wrong to "evade taxes on money earned in your spare time."

In France, the irregular economy is estimated to be 25% of the GNP, and half those officially "unemployed" there are said to be employed unofficially. Sweden's underground is said to be 25% of the whole, Japan's 15%, Israel's nearly a third, and South Africa's fully half.

Irregular economies are probably most important in the most extensively regimented economies. Thus, ironically, the most dramatic demonstrations of the strength of the unchained enterprise are emerging in socialist countries. Some Communist regimes may be staying in power in part because of the economic health they promote by condoning capitalist enterprise.

"In Hungary, Poland and Czechoslovakia," according to *The New York Times*, "the second economy has grown so dominant that many workers . . . devote more time and energy to that sector than to their regular jobs." Two-thirds of Hungary's work force have a second, unofficial job. Private gardening plots representing 15% of Hungary's cultivated land produce a third of its farm products. The official wait for an apartment is ten or twelve years, but intricate private exchanges are often arranged overnight.

Russia's second economy has grown large—perhaps equal to a fourth of its first economy. *Shabashniks*, moonlighting work brigades, hire themselves out, at four or five times the prevailing wage, to construction projects falling behind schedule. At least a quarter of a million Russians are illegally employed in the production of home-brewed vodka.

The economist who has studied America's irregular economy most carefully, Edgar L. Feige of the University of Wisconsin, has estimated that it equaled 26.6% of the measured economy in 1978 and was growing four times faster than the measured economy. About a third of the total is in flatly forbidden activities—drug dealing, prostitution, gambling, fencing stolen goods, and loansharking. Growing and selling marijuana is only one corner of it.

Almost everyone in America is touched by the underground economy. It probably employs 20 million people, including 4 to 6 million illegal immigrants. Every year tens of thousands of Americans are dropping out of the regular economy and joining the irregular one, earning their keep in it, investing their savings in it, and protecting their valuables in it as others do by sending them to Switzerland. In a bank robbery in New York's Chinatown, the thieves bypassed the bank vault and went for the safe deposit boxes, where the real money was.

The IRS believes that self-employed persons, farmers, and

small businesses fail to report about 40% of their incomes. Self-employment is increasing for the first time since the Civil War. Business is making itself small to escape destructive taxes and regulation.

The underground economy is probably the principal economy for many of the poor. Louis A. Ferman, director of research of the Institute of Labor and Industrial Relations, studied participants in the irregular economy in Detroit. "The ability to do irregular work," he told *The Wall Street Journal*, "means the difference between getting by and not getting by for some people . . . others can continue to own their homes that might not otherwise, including many elderly people. Some things, like small appliance repairs, ju* can't be had from regular sources in some places." People excluded by apprenticeship rules in the regular economy learn trades in the irregular economy or use it to ease into full-time self-employment.

Until recently, the irregular economy has been primarily based on cash, but now barter, often easier to conceal from the state, is growing rapidly. Hundreds of barter clubs are being formed around the country. Some, using plastic cards, record complex transactions among thousands of members who contribute to and draw from a pool of services. A dentist "pays" services to other members and "withdraws" meals, legal services, and the like.

But the astonishing growth of irregular economies is only the most visible and best publicized aspect of a much larger phenomenon: entire societies are reshaping themselves, outgrowing their present forms and definitions.

The Italian solution is not just economic; it involves the creation of alternatives for the failed functions of the state— some formal and some highly informal. There are alternative postal services, alternative sanitation services, alternative police and fire services.

Behind the iron curtain, a second society goes far beyond economics. It includes illicit publishing and unauthorized living room theaters. Unofficial "flying" high schools and colleges teach forbidden subjects in blacked-out apartments. An underground Czech publisher issues fifty books a year, typewritten ten carbons at a time or mimeographed, part of a subterranean information network that includes cassette tapes, shortwave radios, and magazines passed hand-to-hand.

In India, a voluntary social activism is flourishing as the political system decays. "The broad institutional framework is in collapse," according to an Indian observer, and several thousand groups in almost all the nation's 350 administrative districts are moving into the vacuum—a dairy cooperative with 400,000 members, groups dedicated to eradicating the caste system and helping its victims, groups involved in reforestation. The editor of the *Indian Express*, a major national newspaper, believes that the cumulative efforts of these sometimes amorphous and quixotic groups are more important than the international aid programs or the social welfare system.

Demographer Nick Eberstadt of the Harvard Center for Population Studies, in an article about the health crisis in the Soviet Union, reminds us of the fact that, while the role of the official health system is most conspicuous in maintaining health, other invisible processes are "of even greater importance." Not just decent meals, he continues, but "the web of personal relationships which can support us against adversity. A mother's care for her baby, a family's attention to its elderly or troubled members, and the will to live which such things inculcate, in an often unnoticed way, do for the health of an affluent nation what a ministry of health could never hope to duplicate."

In Russia there is an official health monopoly, but infant mortality is rising alarmingly and life expectancy declining in part because the invisible "web of personal relationships" has been displaced by the state. Alcoholism is pandemic. The death rate of babies in state-run day care centers is twice as high as that for babies whose families care for them.

Scholars are discovering that there is almost no correlation between spending for medical services and health. Health spending in the United States more than quadrupled between 1965 and 1978, from $39 billion to $192 billion, nearly doubling its share of the GNP, without discernibly improving the health of the nation.

In totalitarian societies, where the state has claimed a monopoly of the public business simply by declaring that the state *is* the society, the distinction between the official society and the "other," unofficial society is plain. In the United States, the borders between the two worlds are not so clear. Nevertheless, there are two Americas, with contradictory values and practices, one that fits the dominant social paradigm perfectly and another that does not fit it at all.

One America is centralized, official, directed, and controlled. The press reports this America extravagantly, and thus the illusion is perpetuated that "official" America—the most centralized and authoritarian institutions that form the visible crust of the society—is the whole society. But there is another reality—a second society characterized by decentralization, self-supervision, independence, autonomy, authenticity, and the redevelopment of forgotten capacities. It is growing up under the petrified structures of the official society just as grass grows up through cracks in concrete.

Author Jane Jacobs, looking out the window of her house in Greenwich Village one day, noticed a little girl about eight years old standing below on the sidewalk. A man, a stranger to the neighborhood, approached the child. It was too soon to see clearly whether the encounter was innocent or not, so Mrs. Jacobs kept watching.

"As I watched from our second-floor window, making up my mind how to intervene if it seemed advisable, I saw it was not going to be necessary. From the butcher shop beneath the tenement had emerged the woman who, with her husband, runs the shop. She was standing within earshot of the man, her arms folded and a look of determination on her face. Joe Cornacchia, who with his sons-in-law keeps the delicatessen, emerged at about the same moment and stood solidly to the other side. Several heads poked out of the tenement windows above, one was withdrawn quickly and its owner reappeared a moment later in the doorway behind the man. Two men from the bar next to the butcher shop came to the doorway and waited. On my side of the street, I saw the locksmith, the first man and the laundry proprietor had all come out of their shops and that the scene was also being surveyed from a number of windows besides ours. That man didn't know it, but he was surrounded."

Mrs. Jacobs concludes, "The public peace . . . of cities is not kept primarily by the police, necessary as police are. It is kept primarily by an intricate, almost unconscious, network of voluntary controls and standards among the people themselves and enforced by the people themselves."

Hayek calls these seemingly spontaneous achievements the products of human action but not of human design. Edmund Burke wrote of collective enterprises "formed by habit and not the sudden jerk of authority." They include mankind's most remarkable accomplishments—language, common law, and anonymous architecture, among others.

The development of language is a complex, continuous, spontaneous collective endeavor in which everyone who uses language participates. Anyone can add to the language—very young people often do—or affirm additions made by others. The language has a corps of self-appointed guardians, but the final authority is so broadly collective as to be impersonal. The result is so complex as to be indescribable. The earliest dictionaries did not even try to encompass the whole language; they listed only unusual words. Today's most nearly complete dictionaries are incomplete from the beginning and obsolete before the ink is dry.

The common law evolved in a similar way. The judge's function was not to make law but to discover law that had been made already—impersonally and collectively—over many centuries. The ruler was the protector of the law, which expressed the common will. Judges "make" law, as Sir Carleton Kemp Allen has said, only in the sense that "a man who chops a tree into logs has *made* the logs." Early codes were not intended to alter the law but merely to record it. International law is still necessarily a "grown" law, a body of law that has evolved organically.

Writers often prepare catalogs of manners, but manners are made by the people who practice them. Some of the world's most admired architecture, Italy's beautiful old farm houses, for example, were designed by no one and, in a sense, designed by the tens of thousands of *contadini* who made them, each generation building on the work of the last.

This kind of spontaneous self-improvement goes on endlessly in most societies and takes dozens of forms. One of the most striking examples of urban renewal is New York City's Soho district. A dozen years ago it was a dark, dying no-man's land. Now it is alive again—one of New York's most desirable neighborhoods. It was a sensible redevelopment, in which the splendid old industrial buildings were adapted to contemporary uses with their character intact. The restoration of Soho took place against the grain of public policy. It was not only not official, it was illegal, and Soho, having succeeded, had to be slowly decriminalized after the fact. But such accomplishments have no place in the dominant paradigm and go largely unnoticed; public policy is formed as if they did not exist.

Scott Burns, in his highly original book *The Household Economy*, sketches some of the probable dimensions of the central institution in the unmeasured "other" unofficial society. He estimates that America's households produce goods and services equal to about a third of the GNP and half of disposable consumer income.

In pre-industrial America, the average household produced three-fourths of what the family needed. Industrialization stood that ratio in its head, but now the household is ascending again. They are not economic units in the orthodox sense, but they produce goods and services which, taken together, have vast economic value.

Some of the figures are astonishing. In 1981, more people

built their own houses with their own hands than hired contractors to build them. Owner-builders started 148,000 units, compared to 122,000 units owners hired contractors to build. Nearly 85% of the nation's householders do some or all of their own maintenance and remodeling.

If a family hires a contractor to build a house, the transaction becomes part of the GNP. If they build it themselves, it becomes part of the unmeasured, unrecorded "other" society: it has no official existence.

In 1980, 43% of the nation's 34 million households produced some or all of their own vegetables in backyards or rooftop gardens. The average plot covers 750 square feet and produces 772 pounds of vegetables worth $497 at retail. There are 2 million community gardens in the big cities.

Students of self-care have concluded that sensible health practices—exercise, a balanced diet, reasonable, regular sleep—are the principal cause of good health and, on the average, lengthen life by thirty years. People use professional resources for guidance in these practices only 1% of the time. They guide themselves and they guide each other.

An independent British task force headed by John Fry concluded that the sick people they surveyed treated themselves 63% of the time by doing something and another 16% by deliberately doing nothing. "Without self-care," the group concluded, "any system of health care would be swamped."

Nine out of ten breast cancers are discovered by the women themselves, and early detection is vital to successful treatment. (Half the major cancers, according to the American Cancer Society, could be prevented if people changed behaviors they themselves already control.)

More and more devices beyond the thermometer are being developed to enhance and extend self-care—home pregnancy tests, home throat cultures and urine-testing sets, otoscopes, and dozens of others. Sales of the industry producing devices for self-care are growing 20% a year and expected to exceed $400 million by 1985.

Chronic disease is cared for principally at home. Fewer than

5% of adult chronic disease patients are in institutions. Diabetics have been caring for themselves for years. Self- and family-care of stroke patients proves at least as effective as that provided by institutions. Hemophilia is being successfully treated at home.

The number of home births is increasing rapidly after decades of decline as evidence mounts that they are at least as safe as hospital births and freer from complications.

More people are making their own clothes again, canning food, making music at home, and learning how to represent themselves in simple legal proceedings.

Families and friends perform a wide range of services for one another without thinking of themselves as part of a vast, decentralized welfare system. They lend money to each other; provide temporary housing for each other. They are a primary source of information about jobs and a principal pool of venture capital for small businesses. They provide transportation, meals, clothing, and child care, and offer information and instruction on hundreds of subjects from sex to astrophysics. They arbitrate disputes, provide psychotherapy and recreation.

Martin D. Lowenthal, associate director of the Social Welfare Institute, speaks of this "social economy" in which friends perform valuable services for one another without charge, and which permits people to get by comfortably with little cash income. Yet such people may be called unemployed. "Too many public programs," he says, "especially ones involving housing and care for the young and old, ignore or even destroy the networks that people erect to take care of themselves."

These undirected, uncontrived, informal, person-to-person relationships (the British call them the "personal sector") are the basis of a workable society. Societies are strong when custom engages the full energy and imagination of the people in self- and mutual-support, not when "official" services are substituted for these more primary interpersonal support systems.

But there are limits to the reach of spontaneous action, and complex societies such as ours must go far beyond them. "Indeed," write Lowell S. Levin and Ellen L. Idler in *The Hidden Health Care System,* "it would be difficult to see how anyone could put such pluralistic groups to any unified purpose." There is also a need for more consciously contrived common efforts, for the more deliberately formed institutions of the independent sector.

14

Anatomy of the Independent Sector

"Society performs for itself almost everything that is
ascribed to government."

—Thomas Paine
The Rights of Man

In spite of a half century of imprisonment in a limiting definition of its possibilities, the independent sector has become, almost without nurture, a vast, sprawling, intricate, uncharted
and unchartable world.

America's overall institutional landscape is quickly
sketched. There are 230 million people, 60 million families,
and an untold number of circles of friends. At the other end of
the institutional spectrum, there are one federal government,
fifty state governments, and, at the last official count, 82,637
local governments of various shapes and sizes—cities, counties, special districts of several kinds—principally school districts. There are about 13 million commercial entities, ranging
from bootblacks, pushcart peddlers, and chimneysweeps to
giant corporations. And running through and among and
around all these like glue are the institutions of the independent sector.

This Third Sector is a rich stew of organizations, formal and
informal, good and bad, sensible and sentimental, serious and
silly, big and little, imaginative and conventional. The variety
of purposes of independent organizations is staggeringly diverse. There is no generally recognized method of classifying

its primary activities, but tentative attempts list hundreds. The preservation of historical sites, suicide prevention, financial counseling, loans and advice to small business, disaster relief, literacy training, testing personal traits and abilities, the recognition of personal heroism, penology, character building, adoption services, educational broadcasting, scientific-data exchange, the promotion of athletic excellence, civil defense, legal aid, business research, and a wide variety of health-care, health-testing and health-maintenance activities are only a few.

The independent sector is by no means provincial. It reaches into every corner of the globe. The State Department calls international independent agencies "NGOs" (nongovernmental organizations) and lists hundreds of them. They distribute money, medical services, supplies and equipment; they provide technical assistance of all kinds; they arrange exchanges of cultural and scientific information.

The configuration of the independent sector is vastly more complex than that of either the government sector or the commercial sector.

Some of its entities are highly organized, and on the surface are difficult to distinguish from businesses. Others take special pride in their lack of formal structure.

Some independent organizations depend almost entirely on money contributions; others refuse to accept them.

Some make extensive efforts to enlist volunteers; others are staffed entirely by professionals.

Some independent groups are international; others limit their activities to a single city block.

Many are very large; most are very small.

Nor are their aims consistent. For example, there are agencies that provide abortion services and actively promote their use, while others try to discourage abortion and lobby for its abolition.

Some independent organizations seek government support; others reject it.

Some independent organizations are very old (Harvard was founded in 1636); many were formed yesterday.

Sometimes their methods are simplistic and naive; sometimes they are highly complex and sophisticated.

The forms and functions of independent action in America are so diverse that any generalization about the abilities and possibilities of the Third Sector is bound to be misleading.

It is sometimes said to be more inventive than the other two sectors, and while this is not true of all its entities, it is demonstrably true of many.

The sector clearly has a remarkable agility: a new entity can be formed overnight and disbanded when its job is done.

It has unusual geographic flexibility. Whereas government agencies normally operate within rigidly defined jurisdictions, independent agencies create jurisdictions of their own, assuming whatever geographic shape their particular mission suggests—local, regional, or international.

The Third Sector, because it can operate without consensus, has traditionally been a haven for minority concerns and activities. The civil rights movement was, in the beginning, necessarily an independent sector movement.

The sector provides platforms where unconventional views can be explored, debated, and offered for consideration to the larger public on such subjects as voluntary sterilization, school decentralization, and the advocacy of alternative forms of government.

The independent sector constitutes this society's cutting edge. It is the sector to which even the alienated can belong, and in which the powerless can begin to build a sense of power.

Perhaps most important of all, it has provided the principal channel by which any citizen, regardless of age, race, affluence, or ability, can act on his concerns in any peaceful way he chooses.

Thus, the Third Sector utilizes human qualities that our commercial and governmental institutions, necessary as they are, cannot so readily exploit. It is the channel through which citizens can become most fully involved.

Without the sector's complex enabling machinery, the human qualities most essential to building a good society—caring, resourcefulness, creativity—would have no ready outlet.

Because so little is known about the sector, estimates of its size have been correspondingly relaxed.

The Third Sector comprises a number of specialized subsectors, some much more sharply defined and visible than others. The part of the sector that shows seems to be all there is.

By far the most visible subsector of the independent sector is that supported by donations. This charitable or philanthropic subsector consists of the three-quarters of a million formally organized agencies that raise money from the public.

This familiar group includes nearly half a million churches, mosques, and synagogues; about 1500 colleges and universities, with a total enrollment of about 2 million; a parallel system of private and parochial elementary and secondary schools with 5 million students; 3300 voluntary hospitals; 6000 museums; 1100 symphony orchestras; 5500 libraries and 37,000 community services agencies affiliated with the United Way of America.

In 1981, Americans contributed $53.62 billion to the charitable subsector; about 90% came from individuals, the rest from foundations and corporations. The largest single chunk of the money, about 46%, went to religious bodies.

There are about 22,000 American foundations with assets totaling about $40 billion. In 1981, 23.4% of the nation's 2.5 million corporations gave $3 billion to independent sector organizations—1.29% of all pre-tax corporate profits. This percentage has hovered close to 1% for as long as it has been compiled.

In addition to money, in 1981, 84 million Americans gave 8.4 billion hours, worth $64.5 billion, to these charitable groups.

Regrettably, the philanthropic subsector of the much larger independent sector is almost universally mistaken for the whole. But these charitable agencies, visible in part simply because they must continuously solicit money from the public, constitute only a fraction of the sector and have a much smaller capacity for growth than the sector as a whole. They are atypical in a number of important ways.

First of all, agencies of this subsector are sustained primarily by money contributions, while most of the independent sector is not.

Moreover, they are usually staffed by professionals; volunteers are used primarily as fundraisers or policymakers. It is much less common for volunteers to be involved in any direct helping capacity. The agencies of the philanthropic subsector raise money from the public with which they hire professionals to administer some social or health or educational service to clients—often primarily middle-class clients. It is only marginally unfair to say that these charitable agencies are hard to distinguish from government agencies and, in fact, they are increasingly financed by government. The agencies under the United Way umbrella in the major cities receive an average of 46% of their support from the government. In New York City the figure is 71%.

Lowell Levin and Ellen Idler write of the philanthropically supported health agencies: "The voluntary association has become, in effect, a quasi-official social resource in health, fixed firmly in the system, politically voluntary, but structurally complementary to the official health structure." The same could be said of most of the agencies in the philanthropic subsector.

This subsector has received roughly 2% of the GNP for many years. Because it is cash-intensive, its rate of growth has necessarily been slow. In fact, it is widely perceived as "threatened" or "endangered," something to be rescued from extinction or preserved, like historic monuments.

E. M. Forster once mocked the Quakers for opposing Armaggedon with philanthrophy, and any suggestion that these entities might remedy the great systemic failures of the modern welfare state seems equally absurd.

In the first place, their leaders do not have any sharply developed sense of independent identity; most of them see their agencies as instruments of the state. One respected spokesman for the philanthropic subsector, Waldemar A. Nielsen, although he confuses the subsector with the whole, states the matter clearly in his book *The Endangered Sector:*

"The old era of *laissez-faire* pluralism is therefore beyond any doubt past. The new era is one of socialization and politicization, of complexity and interconnection. A time of planned, governmentalized, officially subsidized and guided pluralism is upon us. Nonprofit institutions, as one element in a society in radical transition, will never again be the same in status, relative scale, function or autonomy.

"Most of the Third Sector—including all of its great institutionalized elements except the churches—must henceforth live within the embrace of, and to a significant degree as dependents and instruments of, government. That situation already and unmistakably obtains, and there is no plausible basis for supposing that it can be reversed—or indeed that either party to the relationship wishes to reverse it. The leaders of most of the major categories of Third Sector institutions want more government money, not less, and are fully prepared to accept the regulatory consequences."

Thus, Ronald Reagan's half-informed exhortation in the first year of his administration that "private initiatives" pick up some of the pieces of the crumbling welfare state produced a complicated comedy of overlapping errors. White House aides were said to be "optimistic that charitable giving will increase to fill the gap left by the budget cuts." But an even wider gap divided that expectation and the judgment of the leaders of the charitable agencies themselves.

The institutions to which the appeal seemed to be addressed, thinking, as they necessarily do, primarily in terms of money, thought the president meant they should raise enough money to expand to whatever extent the government did not—and probably that is what he did mean. In any case, representatives of the sector began to tell anyone who would listen that this was not a realistic expectation but a laughable one.

C. William Verity, the chairman of the committee Reagan had appointed to find alternatives to federal programs, told the press, "It is unrealistic to expect us to fill what is not just a gap but a chasm."

The New York Times reported: "Leaders of private charities say they will not be able to meet President Reagan's challenge to raise enough money for the needy and provide enough volunteers to offset cuts in federal social programs."

The Roman Catholic archbishop of Detroit went to Washington to tell a congressional committee that charities could not begin to fill the gap in federal aid.

"I can assure the president," wrote the head of the National Council of Jewish women, "that volunteer resources are not sufficient for the tremendous task he is proposing."

And Brian O'Connell, president of Independent Sector, an organization with a name much broader than its membership, said patiently, "It would be a disservice to the president and the public to exaggerate what voluntary organizations can do."

After the dust had settled it appeared that when Reagan had called on the independent sector to help roll back the welfare state, it had responded that it could not and would not, and moreover begged him to stop threatening to cut its federal grants.

It is true that philanthropy is reaching the limits of its utility in modern society, but that truth has been construed to mean that the whole independent sector has no future. The sector has responded honestly with the only voice it has, but that voice represents only a small part of the whole, which, with 7 million entities or more, is perhaps ten times larger than its

philanthropic subsector. The larger sector uses resources that
are abundant and expandable; it is not static but growing rapidly, moving into many new fields; and it is expanding most
rapidly in fields traditionally thought to be "natural" government monopolies.

Mutual-aid groups, for example, which use no money or
nearly none, seem to be expanding geometrically. Their national clearing house estimates that 10 million Americans are
now involved in 700,000 to 800,000 such groups.

The medical profession is tending more and more to con-
centrate its attention on acute care, leaving a vacuum in rehabilitation and the continuing care of chronic disease or of temporary or permanent disability—medical, psychological, or
social—for mutual-aid groups to fill. Alcoholics Anonymous is
the largest and best-known of these groups, but there are organizations that help arthritics, mastectomy patients, stutterers,
schizophrenics, and the parents of dwarfs or Vietnam veterans.
Forward Face helps persons suffering from craniofacial diseases. There is a group called Parents of Murdered Children.
There is one made up of persons stricken by Huntington's disease, an hereditary disease that usually strikes during middle
age and is eventually fatal. There are associations for the blind,
for cancer patients, for burn victims, and for those afflicted by
heart disease, diabetes, and epilepsy.

The mutual-help movement, which has been expanding
since the sixties, is international. There are hypertension clubs
in Yugoslavia, associations of relatives of mental patients in
Austria, and conscious-raising groups for children in England.

There is an endless number of organizations devoted to less
serious interests. Their unifying relationship is some common
object of curiosity, enthusiasm, or concern—for example, col-
lectors of antique microscopes and the American Homing Pigeon Association. There are clubs of Soviet immigrants, May-
flower descendants, and feminist vegetarians. Three thousand
music lovers assemble in Chicago at Christmastime and sing
Messiah together. There is the Portland Friends of Cast Iron

Architecture, the Theatre for Revolutionary Satire, and the Guild of English Hand Bellringers.

The Flat Earth Society, with 1500 members, insists that the earth is a "circular disk surrounded by a barrier of ice that man has never penetrated." (Charles K. Johnson, its president, told an interviewer, "If the earth were a globe, the 100-mile-long Suez Canal would have a center hump 1666 feet higher than each end. Of course, that's not so.") The members of another group, very loosely organized, speak only in words in one syllable. There is the American Tentative Society, pledged to remind the world that nothing is certain. There are both birthing and burial societies.

There is a Society of Independent Scholars, whose membership includes the growing number of men and women who do serious scholarly work outside the academy. There is a Committee for the Elimination of Death. There are 2000 backyard wildlife habitats, certified by the National Wildlife Federation. There is HALT—Help Abolish Legal Tyranny—to protect citizens from the legal profession.

One of the fastest-growing forms of mutual-help group is the block association. New York City has at least 10,000 of them in the five boroughs and may have as many as 14,000.

Another rapidly growing subsector comprises agencies that are not money-intensive but time-intensive. This subsector, which uses primarily the contributed time of skilled or semiskilled persons to act on the public business, is one of the oldest forms of independent action. It is said that half the signers of the Declaration of Independence were volunteer firemen, and in New York State volunteer fire companies still outnumber paid companies nine to one.

The National Ski Patrol, founded by an injured skier in 1938, has 23,000 members trained in rescue and first aid. The Civil Air Patrol, with more than 60,000 members and 7000 planes, is a major resource in air search and rescue and disaster relief. In 1980, members of the CAP flew 14,424 hours in 1175 search missions.

The National Speleological Society sponsors the National Cave Rescue Commission, whose ten regional rescue organizations assemble teams as necessary—usually about forty a year—from the society's 5700 members.

Suicide prevention centers in the major cities are staffed by volunteers; rape crisis centers are another new, time-intensive form. In Chicago, Arc Rehab Corporation, staffed by volunteer architecture students, offers low-cost architectural know-how to families and community groups renovating old homes or transforming old factories. A school volunteer program in Florida involves 77,000 volunteers. Five thousand volunteers read books into tape recorders for Recordings for the Blind.

Some of the mainline independent agencies have learned to use volunteers for tasks that go far beyond fundraising. Years ago, the National Association for Infantile Paralysis managed its historic immunization of almost the whole population of the United States against polio with thousands of health professionals working as volunteers.

In 1959, in the most extensive study of life and death ever undertaken, the American Cancer Society enrolled and trained 68,000 volunteers to reach a million Americans. The study covered six years, but the volunteers' follow-up efforts were 98% successful. One volunteer commandeered a game warden's helicopter to pursue a subject into the Arizona desert. That study unmistakably linked smoking and cancer and pointed the way to preventing nearly a third of cancer deaths.

In the fall of 1982 the ACS launched a second study with 1.2 million subjects, this time involving 100,000 volunteers. Without volunteers, this study would have cost more than a hundred million dollars, but it is unlikely it would have been undertaken at all.

The most impressive increases in efforts by volunteers are in areas traditionally governmental. Ten years ago, citizens' crime-watching groups were scattered and somewhat suspect. Now there are 5 million members in 20,000 communities nationwide. Many communities served by them report radically reduced crime rates. In Detroit, there are Neighborhood Watches on 4000 of the city's 12,000 residential blocks. In New York city, there are 70,000 trained block watchers and 7000 unpaid uniformed auxiliary police officers who patrol the streets and subways with nightsticks and handcuffs but without guns. The Guardian Angels, a group of inner-city teenagers who patrol the New York subways, have enlisted hundreds of members and is spreading to other cities.

In Phoenix, volunteer auxiliary police are screened as carefully as their paid counterparts, then trained and tested. They must work sixteen hours a month; some work forty or more. The time they contribute every year is estimated to be worth $600,000.

A thirty-five-member commune called Plenty operates a free ambulance service in the South Bronx, one of New York's toughest neighborhoods. In Columbia, Maryland, the Columbia Commuter Bus Corporation, a volunteer-run independent organization, operates seventeen daily buses between Columbia and downtown Washington.

As municipal services deteriorate, the development of alternative services, whether volunteers are used extensively or not, has become a major frontier of the independent sector. According to *The New York Times,* ever since that city's fiscal crisis erupted in 1975, there has sprung up "a kind of second track in the delivery of services." Block associations have hired private guards, and about 550 privately arranged buses bypass the decaying subway system. The responsibility for maintaining some parts of New York's parks has been assumed by private groups from a paralyzed Parks Department.

Other independent groups are the primary force in the resettlement of refugees, the people governments have failed or rejected. Between 1975 and 1980, more than 300,000 refugees from Southeast Asia were resettled in the United States—a coordinated effort by dozens of independent agencies. Then came the Cubans and Haitians, and another 135,000 were reestablished here. Arco Products sponsored the rescue ship

Arcuna, which pulled 1000 "boat people" from the South China Sea. In New York, hundreds of volunteer tutors teach English to refugees. In Minneapolis–St. Paul, a coalition of church and community groups brought together by the American Refugee Committee found housing and work for 9000 Laotian refugees.

Sixty years ago, the Oregon legislature decreed that any child in a private school would be considered a truant. Recently half the parents of public school children told the Gallup poll they would prefer to send their sons and daughters to private schools if they could afford them. Private pre-college education for students of modest means is increasing as public school enrollments decline. (Chicago's public schools have twice the enrollment of the city's Catholic schools, but a hundred times the number of administrators.) Polls show the highest rate of dissatisfaction with the urban public schools among inner-city black people, and the enrollment in black-run private schools is increasing. In 1960, Ruby Bridges, then six years old, endured threats and insults to enroll as the first black student in New Orleans' desegregated schools. Twenty years later she took her three children out of the public school system and enrolled them in a parochial school.

Businesses contribute about 5% of the total income of the philanthropic subsector—about a fifth of what these organizations receive from government. In spite of sustained efforts to increase this corporate giving, the amount has been fairly static for years.

But other forms of corporate involvement are growing rapidly. Many of the larger corporations encourage employees to take on community service projects on company time. A few offer sabbatical years for the purpose. The full dimensions of this form of corporate support are not known, but it is large and growing.

Today another form of business social action is increasing: corporations are acting *directly* on public problems, not through mercenaries, surrogates, or third parties. Thousands of businesses of all sizes are involved in this way, and their efforts take hundreds of forms.

Control Data in Minneapolis may be the nation's most involved corporation. The company has deliberately located six plants in stricken inner-city areas and all have succeeded. It has given remedial education, counseling, and paid work experience to 5000 inner-city young people.

Through a leasing subsidiary, it provides used cars to recently released ex-offenders on liberal credit terms to expand the range of job opportunities. It developed Employees Advisory Resource, a twenty-four-hour hotline counseling service. Norbert Berg, who heads the group which develops these initiatives and looks for new ones, told an interviewer: "The pressing issue of the day is finding jobs for people. We start there." The company rehabilitated row houses in Baltimore and sold them back to community residents at cost.

In 1978, Control Data formed a consortium of fourteen business and religious organizations called City Venture Corporation to plan and manage enterprises in depressed urban communities.

IBM has operated a plant in the Bedford-Stuyvesant section of Brooklyn for fourteen years, making components for its most powerful computer. It began as a social experiment, but in seven years the plant was working as well as other IBM facilities.

Digital Equipment makes all its half-inch tape drives in a plant in an impoverished neighborhood in Springfield, Massachusetts. In Lincoln, Nebraska, Kawasaki, the Japanese motorcycle maker, lent some of its employees to the city to rehabilitate the city hall instead of laying them off.

The New York Times describes Minneapolis as "a thriving urban center where virtually every civic improvement has been planned and paid for by the prosperous corporations that have their headquarters there," including half a billion dollars in new construction and rehabilitation creating thousands of jobs.

A group of New York businessmen, acting through a Jobs

Cooperative at the Grand Street Settlement House, find jobs in their own firms for people on public assistance.

Conoco sponsors a program to train prison inmates as deep-sea divers. The program began when a Conoco executive guessed that imprisonment might reinforce the qualities the job requires—composure under stress in closely confined conditions.

Lincoln National Life Insurance is rehabilitating housing in Fort Wayne, its headquarters city. Beginning with six square blocks, Lincoln National, acting through a subsidiary created for the purpose, rehabilitated the houses and rented them to low-income families for $125 a month. After the first five years, the tenants bought the houses for a dollar and assumed the mortgage at below-market interest. The first project completed, the company has begun two more covering twelve square blocks.

The Campbell Bosworth Machinery Company is a small leather-goods machinery manufacturing company in Queens, New York. It trains and places high-school dropouts in the use of leather-goods machinery.

Another large and growing form of business involvement is the assumption of traditionally governmental tasks—principally education. As public school programs have declined in effectiveness, efforts in this area have grown until business spends $30 billion a year for education—an amount equal to the total of public spending for colleges and universities.

For example, AT&T spends $6 million a year for training in basic mathematics and writing with a continuous enrollment of 14,000. Continental Illinois National Bank and Trust Company gives a twenty-week course in spelling, punctuation, and grammar to all new employees. Polaroid decided ten years ago that the remedial and bilingual programs given in public schools didn't meet their needs and provides programs of its own. IBM retrains routinely and continuously in order to avoid layoffs—a contemporary form of the efforts to "regularize" employment that business developed in the twenties.

Some of the very largest and most effective entities of the

independent sector fit least comfortably the dominant definition of what it is proper and possible for nongovernmental
agencies to do, and thus have been consigned to a kind of
limbo in the public consciousness.

Most of their leaders would blanch at the suggestion that
they were somehow engaged in charity, and few of these organizations, in spite of their impressive achievements, depend on
contributed funds. They are some of the best models of what
the independent sector could become.

The American Arbitration Association was established in
1926 in New York City to promote the settlement of disputes
by voluntary methods. Working through twenty-four regional
centers, it provides a list of 50,000 qualified arbitrators, who
often serve without pay, from which the disputing parties
make mutually acceptable choices. The association constitutes
a substantial growing alternative system of justice, handling
about 50,000 arbitration cases a year plus services in media-
tion, conciliation, election, and other methods of voluntary
dispute settlement. The association is nonprofit, but wholly
self-supporting from the nominal fees for the services it provides.

Blue Cross–Blue Shield is an independent organization, or,
more accurately, a national federation of local health and hospital prepayment organizations. Blue Cross began in Texas in
1929 when Baylor University's hospital agreed to guarantee a
group of teachers up to twenty-one days in a semiprivate room
if each paid $6 a year. Blue Shield was added in 1939 to cover
doctors' fees in the same way. Now there are about seventy
Blue Cross–Blue Shield plans, with 86 million subscribers. In
1980, the plans paid out $25.6 billion for care to their subscrib-
ers, well over half as much as the total of American philanthropy that year. Most hospitals participate, as do most of the
nation's doctors. (Blue Cross–Blue Shield, under federal and
state contracts, administers parts of the Medicare and Medicaid programs.)

The Teachers Insurance and Annuity Association was
founded by the Carnegie Endowment for the Advancement of

Teaching to provide pensions for college faculty members. The companion College Retirement Equities Fund was added in 1952. Today, 3500 colleges and universities are involved; 715,000 individual participants are accumulating retirement benefits and 117,000 are receiving them.

The plan pre-dated social security by seventeeen years. Its benefits, like social security's, are fully vested and thus portable from one job to another. But, unlike social security, the plans are fully funded. The combined assets of the two programs totaled more than $20 billion in 1982. Since the plans were established, they have paid out $7.5 billion in benefits.

Electricity of a lethal voltage flows through nearly every house and workplace. Yet, even as the per capita use of electricity increases, the number of deaths associated with electricity is low and declining—about five per million of population per year. The central agency in the protective network that produces this remarkable result is Underwriters Laboratories (UL). Founded in 1894 by the insurance industry as electricity began to be widely used, it is now independent. UL develops safety standards primarily for electrical products, then tests and certifies that products are produced to conform to these standards or to standards developed by others. In 1979, UL examined more than 50,000 products, conducted more than 275,000 factory inspections, and issued 2.2 billion labels for products that met its standards. UL is entirely supported by fees for the services it provides.

UL is one of hundreds of agencies developing standards in a variety of fields—a highly complex, largely voluntary undertaking as old as the industrial era, guided by another voluntary agency—the American National Standards Institute. There are now about 30,000 recognized standards in the United States. Every year thousands of people, mostly volunteers, working through organizations such as the American Society for Testing Materials, the American Society of Mechanical Engineers, and 400 others, spend millions of hours developing new standards or revising old ones. There are standards for oil viscosity. There are several standards ensuring that light bulbs fit sockets

and film fits cameras. There are uniform shoe sizes, battery
sizes, shirt sizes, utensil sizes, eyeglass specifications—all developed by a complex process that produces consensus standards that are at least acceptable to all the groups affected by
them. These voluntarily developed consensus standards are
more workable than those mandated by authorities because,
like language and common law, the affected groups have been
fully involved in their development.

The National Fire Protection Association published Standards for Grading Town Public Fire Protection in 1903, which
has evolved over the years into the complex grading system
that insurance companies use to set fire insurance rates.

There are 130 mutual life and health insurance companies in
the United States, with assets totaling more than $300 bil-
lion—half again as much as the assets of the 1200 stock companies. The assets of the mutual companies providing property
and casualty insurance total nearly $50 billion.

To independent sector organizations like these could reasonably be added the 7000 farm cooperatives, some of them
marketing cooperatives and some so-called supply cooperatives, buying and reselling feed and fertilizer. The largest has
sales of almost $4 billion. There are 9000 other cooperatives, of
which consumer cooperatives are the most familiar, but there
are also fishing cooperatives, artificial insemination cooperatives, craft cooperatives, and dozens more. There are independent economic research agencies—The Brookings Institution,
the Conference Board, the National Bureau of Economic Research.

But such subsectors of the independent sector, formidable as
they are, have little visibility and no voice. They are the least
self-conscious of our social entities. They are strong because
they are autonomous and decentralized. They set their own
priorities. The question is whether they, or entities like them,
would or could be mobilized into concerted national action on
unemployment, retirement security, and the other problems of
an industrial society.

15

Healing America

"It is a remarkable and depressing fact that the vast expansion of the economic activities of the State has not been based on rational analysis."

George Stigler

The healing of America will require a sustained, systematic expansion of the independent sector deep into the domain now considered the territory of government. That, in turn, will depend on rehabilitating the idea, abandoned in the thirties, of concerted action, national in scope but outside government, to provide stability and security. Our sense of national community apart from the state must somehow be restored.

There is no more important decision, or set of decisions, in a modern society than how it divides the necessary collective tasks among the institutions that are part of it. A good society—a sensible society—could be defined as one in which responsibility flows to whatever entity is best able to assume it.

This process has worked very badly—perversely—in the United States during the last half century. We have assigned social responsibility on the basis of estimates of the capacities of various institutions that history is proving to have been tragically mistaken.

The misallocation of responsibility has been exaggerated by another disturbing tendency. America's most ambitious institutions tend to be the least effective, while its most effective institutions tend to be the least ambitious. The federal government has an incomplete sense of its limitations; the independent sector has an incomplete sense of its strengths.

Thus government continues to grow large by default. Because the independent sector is an ineffective contender for public responsibility, it appears that there is no alternative to the state. What should be a rational process—a fair, fully informed contention for public responsibility—has become one whereby all responsibility tends, sooner or later, to flow to the state. A society with an aggressive government sector and a passive independent sector has no guidance system, no capacity for rational decisionmaking. There is no way to define public necessity, to distinguish vital public functions from frivolous ones. The public business becomes open-ended.

Government has become the primary source of information on the nature and extent of problems that may need public attention and which therapies might relieve them. This is perhaps the government's most dangerous monopoly—its power to define the public business, and to judge the adequacy or inadequacy of extragovernmental approaches to dealing with it.

On April 3, 1944, author Allen Drury, then a *New York Times* Washington correspondent, wrote in his journal: "Taft [Robert A. Taft, U.S. Senator from Ohio, known for years as Mr. Republican] was in, thoughtfully clipping his fingernails with a small pair of scissors as he contemplated the legislative problem. 'Obviously something should be done,' he said in that flat, reasonable voice, 'but I hardly hold with the theory that Congress ought to be turned into an executive agency. Congress is a jury, in a sense, expressing the will of the people and passing on proposals put before it.' "

But for fifty years this jury has heard only the case for expanding the scope and size of government. The process of rationalizing this expansion has become institutionalized. Michael J. Malbrin, in his *Unelected Representatives,* explains how the staff available to Congress, now numbering 20,000, works to "discover 'problems' amenable to legislative fixes." In other words, a small army is searching full time for ways to improve American society by enlarging the state. Two centuries ago, James Madison called this already familiar process, "the old trick of turning every contingency into a resource for accumulating force in the government." There is no effective countervailance. Thus, a valid social impulse has become perverted and destructive.

It is vastly more important to alter the circumstances on which the congressional "jury" acts than the mix of politicians who go to Washington to consider them. Politicians who have no choice but to approve or disapprove proposals for federal action cannot make responsible decisions.

If we devised a system whereby responsibility flowed freely and continuously toward competence and away from incompetence, the responsibilities the federal government would retain would probably be very few. (Peter Drucker wrote some years ago that government has only two clearly superior abilities—waging war and inflating the currency.)

If rationality is to be restored, the independent sector must compete for social responsibility consciously and aggressively. It must again think of itself as American society's essential alternative to the state, as having central rather than peripheral importance. The sector must realize that the survival of this society probably depends on its ability to assume responsibility where the state has failed.

As things stand, the Third Sector has no self-consciousness—or nearly none—no sense of its right relationship to other institutions. There is no sense of its size and scope; it is usually confused with a small, atypical subsector. The Third Sector has no leadership—there are acknowledged and capable leaders of several of its subsectors, but none for the sector as a whole. There is no secretariat, no organizational machinery, no voice, no sense of the necessity of demanding in the name of the public interest the tasks it believes it can best perform.

The preconditions for a renaissance of independent action are largely attitudinal. Three stubborn and disabling suppositions must be overturned: that the sector is obsolete; that it does not function at full capacity because it does not know how; that it is secondary and subordinate to the state.

The image of obsolescence is its principal disability. A *New*

York Times reporter, writing of the newly elected Ronald Reagan's apparent interest in voluntary action, referred to "his constant citing of examples of voluntary acts . . . by private individuals." *The Times* commented, "He views the American past that way, although he has some difficulty recalling specific problems of national scope that were solved by voluntary effort."

That, of course, is the rub. Most people have "some difficulty" believing in the modern relevance of voluntary action. They are moved by their memories of what communities once accomplished together, and are touched by tales of individual acts of mercy. But they cannot imagine the impulse mobilized into effective national action on complex problems. The question is not whether the sector worked in Tocqueville's time, but whether it will work today.

The related supposition—that the sector doesn't act because it doesn't know how—assumes that its limitations are technological, that it has somehow lost its knack. There is thus an endless quest for methodology.

After President Reagan appointed C. William Verity of Armco Steel chairman of his Task Force on Voluntary Initiatives, Mr. Verity, discussing his role with *The Wall Street Journal*, said he believed the president wanted him to "sort of stir the pigeons." A few months later he wrote, "The task force hopes to have one of its greatest influences through Project Data Bank, which identifies highly successful examples of promising private initiatives or public/private partnerships. Through the data bank, the task force hopes to disseminate information that communities can use to develop their own programs."

This will become at least the sixth such data bank or clearing house of independent projects, none of which, so far as I know, has led to any significant imitation of the listed programs. The data banks remain depositories from which withdrawals are rarely made.

The issue is not the discovery of new techniques, but why the Third Sector is failing to apply methods that are already widely known. There is no mystery about the shaping of funded pension plans. There are hundreds of such plans. Methods of training young people and putting them to work are common knowledge. The problem is not technical but structural. The tools are readily available: the problem is that the sector is demoralized, unsure of its legitimacy, lacking a sense of direction and mission.

When President Reagan appeals to the nation "to bring thousands of Americans into a volunteer effort to help solve many of America's social problems," he is carelessly appealing to a faith that was lost fifty years ago and will need to be restored by something more sustained and systematic than a committee to "sort of stir the pigeons."

And Reagan's desperate midterm suggestion that each business hire one unemployed person, a pathetic caricature of what must be done, was greeted with the derision it deserved.

The evidence strongly suggests that there needs to be a doctrine of separation of the independent sector and the state. The sector must see itself not as an instrument of the state but as an alternative to the state. Some of the leaders of its charitable subsector hold out a vision of a comfortable future in the arms of the state, but pluralism becomes a pretense if one sector of a pluralistic polity becomes dependent on another. A chastened, captive, and obedient pluralism is false and meaningless.

The leaders of Poland's Solidarity are taking a final stand on this issue. They are insisting that the state is not the society. When Westerners urged Solidarity's leaders to collaborate with the state to avoid bloody confrontation, Solidarity's Zbigniew Bujah told *The New York Times* in a smuggled interview that collaboration would have made Solidarity "another annex of the totalitarian system, creating only an impression of democracy."

Several years ago, the American Cancer Society, one of the visible giants of the independent sector, resolved officially not to accept federal money. It neither publicized nor concealed the action; its purpose was not confrontation but, according to the language of the resolution, simply to affirm and preserve its distinct and separate identity. The amount of money involved was not large, but, the society said, "a central principle was at issue."

"As a voluntary agency," the resolution read, "we bring quite distinctive strengths to the struggle against cancer. We cannot afford to have that special identity blurred or compromised. We must be able to speak without equivocation and act without hesitation. We must avoid any impression that what we do is in any way secondary, subordinate or supplementary."

Separation of the independent sector from the state need not imply antagonism; the contention for social responsibility need not be acrimonious. But there does need to be a sharp awareness of distinct institutional alternatives. The independent sector is elementally different from the state. Its means are more fragile than the powers of the state to tax and command, but it has other distinctive strengths. The sector cannot succeed until it detaches itself from the state.

Moreover, it should not look to the state for leadership. It was Hoover's view, which I accepted wholeheartedly in an earlier book, that the president should become, *ex officio*, the leader of the independent sector—that it was a central task of government to stimulate independent action.

But history suggests that the sector must generate its own distinctive leadership. Recent presidents have, on the whole, done the sector more harm than good. Nixon liked the ring of the independent-sector rhetoric and made some stirring speeches about "the voluntary way." But he had no real confidence in the sector and his support probably caused as many people to abandon as to embrace it.

When Hoover went down politically, he took the Third Sector with him. And Ronald Reagan's uninformed exhortations are simply confirming the public's impression that the independent sector has a limited role in the modern world.

Nonpolitical movements are common to history—religious movements and the early labor organizations are examples. In the ninety-nine years before 1980, the nation had nineteen presidents; the American labor movement had four. For centuries, independent-sector organizations have somehow "formed" when some need was perceived and grown strong as they mobilized some widely felt concern.

Nor can the independent sector adopt the agenda of the state or imitate its therapies, as Reagan seemed to suggest when he called for a voluntary effort to fill the gap that would result if he succeeded in slowing government growth.

Governments, by and large, choose a particular approach to the solution of public problems. They tend to professionalize the public business, using tax money to hire professionals who patrol the streets, collect the garbage, treat the sick, and counsel the unemployed. In the Keynesian decades the high cost of this methodology was not closely scrutinized. Many saw it as an advantage.

There is a powerful tendency for these monopolistic official organizations to become what one observer calls "inverted." All but forgetting the function that justified their establishment, they exist for the benefit of the professionals who inhabit them, and become their own justification. Every federal program—and there are now literally thousands of them—is successful in the Keynesian sense that money is spent and jobholders employed.

The success of the independent sector will be built on a radically different approach to the public business, one that deprofessionalizes it, that seeks to involve the energies of people and their primary institutions rather than excluding them. The sector will rewrite the agenda of public business, redefine it, and approach its solution in its own, wholly different way.

As these attitudinal preconditions are met, the independent sector can rebuild its capacity to provide stability and security. That process will not take place according to blueprint, but it is possible to imagine the shape it might take.

In September 1942, the Committee for Economic Development was set up "to help businessmen plan for quick reconversion and expanded production, distribution and employment after victory." It promptly set up local committees in most communities of over 10,000 and in some smaller ones— 2900 in all; 60,000 businessmen were said to be involved and, through them, many of the nation's 2 million employers. Each local committee was autonomous—charged to develop its own plan for "more production, sales and jobs" when the war ended, working with other organizations in the community. Twenty-seven national Action and Advisory Committees were organized to help and encourage the local committees.

This CED effort was said to be inspired by Jesse Jones, Roosevelt's wartime secretary of commerce, to counter the national assumption that the Great Depression would resume when World War II was over. In fact, and probably to some unknowable extent because of the work of CED's field division, reconversion moved with a speed that astonished most observers. Three months after the surrender, employment reached 51.7 million, and eight months after that it reached a stunning 58.1 million in spite of vast reductions in federal spending.

But the CED's field division was disbanded soon after. It had bought the cooperation of the existing national business organizations by agreeing to demobilize when the reconversion was finished, and it did. A research division survived and still publishes a stream of studies and policy papers on public issues.

The wartime experience of the CED suggests a model for a sustained national assault on unemployment—a nationally coordinated federation of autonomous local groups with access to national resources of research and know-how.

There is no need for new techniques. Unemployment could be eliminated with ones that are already known—how to identify unemployed persons who do not identify themselves, how to help them understand where they might best fit into the work force, how to help them prepare for it, how to help them find work, how to get it and hold it. There are not hundreds of such efforts, there are thousands. They have not produced a national solution to unemployment because there has not been a widely shared recognition of the urgency of doing so—an awareness that the economy is being destroyed by failing federal efforts to accomplish what an independent effort could do.

The CED's wartime program was built on local action, nationally coordinated. It involved cooperation with other business and nonbusiness groups. It achieved widespread participation. It involved the pursuit of an ambitious goal of the highest importance. But, most important, it involved direct business *action*. Businesses were involved not as amateur philanthropists but as businesses.

The commercial sector's action organizations have for the most part disappeared—a process that began in the thirties and gathered momentum after the war—as businesses have more and more come to accept government's near-monopoly of the public business. The business organizations that remain are almost exclusively factories for turning out policy recommendations. "Action" has come to mean political action. The idea that business might use its national organizational machinery to solve national problems was a casualty of the Keynesian revolution.

But the prevailing idea of corporate citizenship is being revised and enlarged. A dimension of corporate behavior repressed for fifty years is ascending again. The money contributions made by business to the various institutions of the charitable subsector are insignificant and inconclusive, but their potential operational contribution to the elimination of unemployment is large and potentially decisive.

A business that obeys the law, pays its taxes, and supports candidates and causes is accepting a tragically incomplete definition of its role in society.

The price of reasonable freedom of enterprise is the maintenance of full employment, sensibly defined, by means outside government, and that price is not negotiable. If this proposition became widely accepted in the business community, a solution, the details of which are not predictable, would in time emerge. Business need not view this commitment as altruistic, but as justified by hard economic calculus. John Filer, chairman of Aetna Life and Casualty, doesn't like the term "social responsibility." He believes business should "do these things because we have a stake in the long-term health of society." Business pays billions in taxes—more than a trillion dollars since 1929—to support an approach to full employment that does not work and is sustained only by the lack of an alternative.

Imagine an industrial society in which the business community accepts, collectively, the responsibility for reasonably full employment and delivers it. It would not be overtaxed, it would not be inflationary, it would probably not be antibusiness.

An independent movement to minimize unemployment would, as a first step, redefine the problem—unbundle it, convert it from a macroeconomic phenomenon susceptible only to macroeconomic solutions, into its microeconomic elements, subject to action by individual firms. *Who, exactly, is unemployed and for what reason?* Those of us who worked to solve this problem in the late sixties rediscovered what decades of macroeconomic thinking had caused us to forget: that each person's predicament is unique and demands an individualized response. Men and women are unemployed or unemployable for many reasons, among them fear, prejudice, misunderstanding, misinformation, ill health, hostility, miseducation, and isolation. The present unemployment numbers are nearly useless as guides to helping these people.

An independent full-employment effort would primarily involve smaller businesses, for this is where most new jobs are formed. David L. Birch of the Massachusetts Institute of Technology found that in the 1970s, two-thirds of all new jobs were formed by firms with twenty or fewer employees, and four-fifths were in firms with a hundred or fewer employees—mostly in service industries. Larger businesses can help with technical and moral support, and community groups with essential support services, but a definitive solution to involuntary unemployment will depend on smaller businesses.

Success would depend on enlisting the sustained support of large numbers of the nation's 2 million corporations, 10 million proprietorships, and 1 million partnerships. Smaller firms have overwhelming public sympathy. In one recent survey, for example, the respondents gave small business higher marks for honesty, dependability, and integrity than any other group, including organized religion. In another survey, 68% said big business had too much power, while small business was at the top of the list of groups perceived as having too little.

A national independent effort would involve the formation of new organizations as well as new networks and coalitions of existing ones. Mutual-help groups made up of jobless or of employed men and women reaching out to help those left behind (in the spirit of the early years of the labor movement) would be an important element. The nation's business-, economic-, and policy-research agencies could provide guidance and information.

Action on unemployment will have to be concerted action. A single business that invests resources of money and manpower into community action compromises its competitive position. It isn't accidental that the most public-spirited companies are most often found in the least competitive industries.

"The result," says former CED chairman William C. Stolk, "is that business generally proceeds by the lowest common denominator of industry action—or inaction. Government then has to take over. . . . Business pays the bill, which is almost always higher than if business had done the job in the first place. . . . This is self-defeating. And it isn't too difficult to find a better way. The machinery is already in place—industry or trade associations. What we have to do is turn them around: convert them from rear-guard defenders of the status quo into instrumentalities of collective industry action in the public interest.

"The industry association is the place where corporate busi-

ness executives can bring their proposed action programs—
sort out who does what—decide on a fair apportionment of the
costs—and work out a detailed industry plan and timetable for
solving the problem."

Some part of the unemployment problem will forever elude
the reach of independent action—that part which is policy-induced. Independent organizations can mitigate the effects of
policy-induced unemployment; they could never wholly eliminate them. But an independent full-employment movement
could, in time, become a powerful voice in legislative reform.

A movement that had achieved solid results in improving
the system would win an uncommon credibility and influence
in the national debate. The wartime CED model had two
branches—the field division, or active branch, and the research division, or policy branch. Had both survived, each
would have powerfully reinforced the work of the other.

There are some serious stirrings in the direction of concerted
national independent action on unemployment. Robert Kilpa-
trick, president of Connecticut General Life Insurance Company, announced the intention of the Business Roundtable to
go beyond policy statements and work with other community
groups to solve such national problems as unemployment and
urban decay. Harvard's John Dunlop, former secretary of
labor, is coordinating a high-powered Labor-Management
Group to "search for voluntary solutions to a wide range of
issues, such as how to create new and expanded job opportunities. . . ."

The heads of more than a hundred insurance companies of
all sizes announced their intention "to direct a share of their
resources nationwide toward grappling with unemployment,
particularly among minority youth." *The New York Times*
wrote that the larger business world would see the commitment as significant "because of the influence and wealth of the
industry, which controls $500 billion in assets, employs a mil-
lion people, and for more than a decade has been heavily involved in investing funds and lending executives for programs
in the inner cities."

The companies consciously chose unemployment as a problem that "reaches out to us for priority attention." They agreed to reassess their present efforts, provide training, and work together with community groups.

Another CED chairman, Fletcher L. Byrom, chairman of Koppers Company, said recently, "We cannot legislate the good life; we are going to have to make it for ourselves. Part of the solution is to relearn how to mobilize private interest for the public good."

Substituting an independent .retirement program for the doomed social security system is in one sense simple and in another sense discouragingly difficult. Public confidence in the present system is eroding rapidly. In 1982, a national poll revealed that more than two-thirds of the persons under forty-five who were queried (68%) do not believe social security will exist when they retire.

It is deceptively easy to visualize the form of an independent alternative. The Teachers Insurance and Annuity Association, the nonprofit educational annuity program, is a perfect model. It is a fully funded, portable system. The premiums the members and the colleges that employ them pay into TIAA are invested; they add to the economy's capital stock. The income these investments earn enhances the value of TIAA's retirement benefits. Administrative and "selling" costs are very low.

Similar institutions could be readily established. Such an independent system would be vastly superior in every way to the present unfunded system. Retirement benefits would be several times larger. There would be a much greater flexibility— no need to limit the earnings of retirees. The rate of capital formation would increase dramatically.

The problem of course is this: there is no apparent way to make a transition that would be acceptable to a majority of the participants. The old system could not afford to let its younger participants out. The new system could not afford to assume the unfunded liability of the older participants. It is a dilemma, and the failure to resolve it is sinking the American economy—and with dry land in plain sight. Politicizing retirement, understandable in the thirties' context, was a serious mistake that must somehow be rectified.

The system was then thought to be temporary, necessary for people whose retirement savings had been swept away in the Crash. It was modest in scale, if not in scope, and was intended to be a minimum on which other provisions would be built. Founded at a time when capital accumulation was considered contrary to the public interest, the system was not funded.

The "pay-as-you-go" system, consistent with the Keynesian spirit of the times, diverted money from saving to spending. Over the years, the effect has been to reduce massively the rate of capital formation.

Harvard's Martin S. Feldstein, president of the National Bureau of Economic Research and chairman of the Council of Economic Advisors, who has studied this phenomenon most carefully, has calculated that social security has reduced savings by about 35%. Without this drain America's capital stock would currently be 80% higher. This meant that in 1981, the GNP was $550 billion less than it would have been—$6600 per family.

The figures for individual participants are even more dramatic. If Americans bought private life insurance, health insurance, and annuities with amounts equal to their social security deductions, the earnings of these invested reserves would multiply the value of their retirement benefits.

Peter J. Ferrara, whose book *Social Security: the Inherent Contradiction* presents a comprehensive analysis of the subject, offers several sample calculations. Because the system redistributes benefits somewhat, awarding disproportionately higher benefits to lower-income workers, the advantages of escaping it vary. A person who entered the workforce in 1980 at age twenty-four and earned the maximum taxable income until retirement would, assuming his premiums earned 6% on the average, accumulate a retirement fund of a million dollars, enough to buy a life annuity paying $100,000 a year—more than five times his social security benefits.

At the other end of the scale, a worker who is entering the system now at age eighteen and earning only the minimum wage all his or her life would have a retirement fund of about $300,000, enough to buy a lifetime annuity paying about $29,-000 a year—almost four times the social security benefit.

The break comes at about age forty. People under forty could buy better protection outside the system with the same money. Those over forty could not.

In practice, the system works like a Ponzi scheme or chain letter. The early generations of participants benefit greatly, at the expense of the later ones, until at some point the machinery breaks down. In twenty-five years, assuming social security survives, the tax on younger workers to support the retired will approach 50% of their wages.

The political establishment cannot reform the social security system. It is congenitally incapable of acting responsibly for the long run. The behaviors that are politically inescapable in the short run will sink the economy in the long run.

The health of the system can be marginally improved in only two responsible ways: taxes can be raised or benefits can be reduced. Since both of these alternatives are politically unacceptable, the only solution is an inflationary one.

The independent sector has more latitude. It could set in motion a long-term reform movement that could, in time, succeed.

The eventual substitution of an independent retirement program would involve three overlapping phases:

1. An informational effort designed to make large numbers of people aware of the problem and the alternatives;

2. The formation of an alternative independent program;

3. A movement to devise and promote acceptable ways to transfer participants from the one program to the other.

It would be like building a sound rescue vessel, bringing it alongside a slowly sinking ship, and evacuating the passengers.

The precarious condition of the system must be widely and accurately understood. Politically, the issue is undiscussable, although there are half-whispered expressions of concern as government employees, who have the choice, vote themselves out of the system by the tens of thousands. An educational effort is needed suitable in scale to a problem that threatens all of us. (Perhaps the cost could be financed in part by contributions from rich beneficiaries. In 1982, 130,000 households with incomes exceeding $75,000 a year were receiving social security checks.)

At the same time, we must begin to build the widest possible coalition of profit and nonprofit insurance industry representatives, citizens, and scholars to design an independent alternative to the social security system, and, above all, devise ways to rescue younger participants from the present system without endangering the benefits of the older ones. Professional associations of actuaries, accountants, and attorneys having specialized knowledge could play an important part.

In time, as more and more people are able to visualize an alternative, constructive debate on the transition could commence. Perhaps workers could be permitted to withdraw from the system in groups conforming to the actuarial composition of the whole system, so there would be a fair sharing of the obligations to older members and the high lifetime premiums of younger ones. Perhaps workers could divide their participation, gradually reducing their participation in the unfunded system. Perhaps younger people could buy their freedom, paying a price that would still represent a net improvement in their benefits. Perhaps workers over a certain age could petition for the right to withdraw.

It is an awesome task, the execution of which would take years. But a reform could succeed—if enough people could begin to believe in the possibility of success.

These two issues—stability and security—are the heart of the new independent agenda. Evidence of success in them

would encourage efforts in other fields such as educational reform, crime prevention, conservation, and the substitution of
independent regulatory systems in dozens of areas.

Problems like these are only the beginning of the agenda of
a good society, the practical basis on which other deeper dimensions of community could be explored—common efforts to
relieve loneliness, isolation, and despair, to affirm the essential
brotherhood of man, to begin to build a peaceable world.

But could such great changes really come to pass? There is
evidence that they are already in motion.

16

The Rebirth of Community

> "The people I respect most behave as if they were immortal and as if society was eternal. Both assumptions are false: both of them must be accepted as true if we are to go on eating and working and loving, and are to keep open a few breathing holes for the human spirit."
>
> E. M. Forster
> *Two Cheers for Democracy*

Can it happen here? Is it possible to believe that the independent sector could in time assume responsibility for what are the modern state's largest tasks? It depends whether the independent sector can somehow take on an aggressiveness not now natural to it, sufficient to counter the blind ambition of the political state.

In some degree, it is happening already: a major reshuffling of responsibility among American institutions is well under way.

Revisionist research is moving beyond chronicling the absolute failures of the welfare state and is beginning to document the comparative superiority of nongovernmental institutions.

A private garbage collection firm which operates in 140 communities finds its costs are 25% to 30% lower than those of municipally run services. A Columbia University study of 2000 communities found private garbage collection 30% more economical.

X rays were found to cost twice as much in a city-run hospital as in an independent hospital of similar size. It costs the Veterans Administration 83% more to keep a patient in one of its own nursing homes than in a comparable private one. The

City of Detroit found it was spending $26 to process a $15 traffic ticket. Now, working under a contract, a private clerical firm has reduced that cost to $1.80.

In Rochester, New York, Patricia Brennan guaranteed delivery of first-class letters on the same day for ten cents apiece until the courts found her in violation of the Post Office monopoly and ordered her to stop.

Litigation takes an average of twenty months in the federal court system. (In Los Angeles, the wait for a place on the court calendar is about four years.) The independent alternative to litigation, arbitration, takes on the average 141 days.

Three of New York City's bridges are in dangerous disrepair: the Brooklyn Bridge, the Manhattan Bridge, and the Queensboro Bridge. Three others are in good condition: the Verrazano-Narrows Bridge, the George Washington Bridge, and the Triborough Bridge. The first three are tax-financed and run by the city; the others are user-financed and run by an independent authority.

Thus, the pressure on the dominant social paradigm increases. The belief that the state is best suited by its nature to perform certain essential tasks becomes, as it collides more frequently with reality, harder and harder to sustain. The belief that independent institutions have congenital limitations is losing ground to powerful contrary evidence. Ancient certainties about the proper distribution of social responsibility are being called into question.

In Switzerland, air traffic control is handled by Radio Suisse, an independent nonprofit corporation, and financed by user fees. In Mexico, Radio Aeronautics, set up by the airlines, handled air traffic control until it was nationalized in 1978. The workers struck in protest.

In France, water supply, historically an unregulated private system, is a model of equity and efficiency.

In the United States, there are commercial fire departments in several states. The country's largest is Rural Metro Fire Department, which serves Scottsdale and thirteen other Arizona communities at about half the cost of conventional govern-ment-run services. Bridges seem to be the most "natural" gov-ernment monopoly, but Detroit's 7490-foot Ambassador Bridge to Canada has been privately owned and operated since it was built in 1929.

As the old stereotypes dissolve, attitudes about the distribu-tion of responsibility are changing. Some observers are calling these reassignments of responsibility "structural" approaches to public policy. A scholar calls them the New Institutional-ism.

Forty percent of the nation's bridges and overpasses, 200,-000 structures altogether, are said to be in need of extensive repairs. An increasingly popular solution is to sell them to groups of investors and finance their maintenance through user fees (tolls). In Pittsburgh, city officials are negotiating with U.S. Steel to build a bridge and then rent it to the city.

In California, litigants in civil court cases are hiring retired judges to conduct trials outside the regular court system, but with similar procedures and protections.

New York City is ceding chunks of its parks—skating rinks, parking lots, and golf courses—to independent agencies and corporations for management. The policy is called "load-shed-ding." In Oakland, California, the zoo society has taken over the operation of the zoo.

Private hospital corporations have been managing public hospitals for a dozen years. Now they are buying them out-right.

The 27,000-acre Rainey Sanctuary in Louisiana, the home of snow geese and alligators, is managed by the Audubon Society, but the society leases the natural-gas rights to three oil com-panies under conditions devised to preserve the wildlife.

There are 20,000 "private" communities in the United States, bound together by perpetual covenants in the individ-ual property deeds. Many of them buy basic protection ser-vices from private contractors.

According to Professor Douglas H. Ginsburg of Harvard

Law School, "Large insurance companies would be perfectly capable of insuring the vast majority of the almost 15,000 commercial banks in the United States. Those few banks that were too large for any one insurance company to handle would be insurable through a syndicate. . . ."

There is thus a new willingness to consider comparative institutional capacities objectively—to think what was, a few years ago, unthinkable.

Confidence in independent action, on the rise for more than a century, was devastated between 1929 and 1933. It will take much longer to rebuild it, but the process has already begun. Twenty years ago, the independent sector had no name and no place in the public consciousness. Now scholars are rediscovering it, and books are being written about it. Yale has established an institute to study its past and its possibilities. An organization called Independent Sector has been established; it represents only the sector's philanthropic subsector, but ten years ago there was no organization at all.

The American Enterprise Institute has departed from decades of strictly economic policy analysis and begun to produce some first-rate monographs on aspects of independent action, some ranging far beyond the philanthropic subsector.

And there are signs that Americans are beginning to imagine, however indistinctly, an alternative to the welfare state. When, in 1981, the Roper organization asked, "Where do you think the truly important work in solving our country's problems will be done in the next ten years or so?", 35% said government. But 30%, almost as many, said "private organizations."

The question is only how far and how fast this renaissance of independent action may develop. Americans are withdrawing from politics; they are losing their confidence in economics. Half the people say they do some volunteer work. An eighth say they do it regularly.

While the official economy is stagnating, the underground

economy seems to have boundless vitality. While the philanthropic subsector is not growing, if we knew the facts we
would probably find that the rest of the independent sector is
growing explosively.

Opinion analyst Daniel Yankelovich has found evidence to
suggest that a new, enlarged concept of citizenship is developing. His book *New Rules* calls for "a renewed emphasis on
the social virtues of sharing, giving, committing, sacrificing,
particpating . . . and, above all, a renewed interest in the future." He reports evidence of an emerging "ethic of commitment" that could be the basis for building a better society.

Expressions of the urgent need for a new vision of community are showing up in some unlikely places. Adam Smith's
(George J. W. Goodman's) book *Paper Money* is a disquieting
picture of a world economy careening out of control. He ends
it with a plea, not for altered economic policy but for a restoration of community—"social cohesion, solidarity, personal
intimacy, emotional depth, moral commitment, continuity in
time, a vision of man in his wholeness rather than in one of his
roles."

Flora Lewis, *The New York Times*' columnist on international affairs, wrote in 1981, "Liberals are floundering because
their pursuit of 'the good society,' with its focus on government and money, didn't bring the community together . . . the
answer isn't at hand. The 20th century is ending in a time of
enormous change and it will surely bring changed ideas. But
there are already many signs that the key is the new relation of
the one and the many. . . ."

Perhaps most important, the new generation of technology
may reinforce the growth of the independent sector. The im-
minence of the postindustrial society has been heralded for so
many years that we were entitled to tire of waiting and wonder whether it would ever come at all.

But now it is here. Our society has become information-in-
tensive, and there has been a technological revolution in the
means of processing, transmitting, and storing information. It

is already clear that the electronic revolution and a parallel revolution in factory automation will in time change the face of this society as profoundly as the first, mechanical phase of the industrial revolution.

The particulars of these changes are unpredictable, but their outlines are already evident in some basic social statistics.

For the first time in a century and a half, small towns are growing faster than big cities. Calvin Beale, head of Population Research for the Department of Agriculture and the principal authority on this phenomenon, says the trend began in 1970, when rural growth began to outrun metropolitan growth for the first time since the census of 1820.

This is not an agricultural renaissance. Employment in agriculture continues to decline as mechanization continues. It is industry that is decentralizing, moving out of the cities and into the countryside. In Kansas, for example, 60% to 70% of the new plants are being built in towns of under 50,000.

At about the same time, another elemental social trend reversed itself. Self-employment, which had been declining for more than a century, began to increase faster than conventional employment. People are becoming more independent, outgrowing the "habits of subordination" that Thomas Jefferson feared the factory system would inculcate.

As the electronic means for handling information become cheaper and cheaper, people who work at great distances from each other can be linked electronically as easily as if they were in the same room. Now, more and more, work can be brought to the people. Some of the seemingly intractable social problems that came with industrialization and urbanization may now become more manageable. For more than a century it has seemed that technology and humanity were in conflict. Now it is possible to imagine a society based on high technology *and* a high degree of humanizing decentralization.

This revolution will not force a revival of the independent sector, but it will surely invite, enable, and reinforce that revival. It will give greater momentum to society's centrifugal tendencies—there will be more smaller communities, where human needs and relationships will be clearer. At the same time, communities can be linked more effectively than ever before: a commentator on the Tylenol poisonings estimated that 85% of America knew about it within an hour of the first media reports.

Local concerns will become more manageable, but informed, concerted national action on national problems will become more practical as information flows more freely.

In the end, a good society is not so much the result of grand designs and bold decisions, but of millions upon millions of small caring acts, repeated day after day, until direct mutual action becomes second nature and to see a problem is to begin to wonder how best to act on it.

And, if someday America succeeds in reviving its sense of community, we will surely wonder in retrospect how we ever thought we could sustain a good society without individual effort.

Acknowledgments

I have incurred many intellectual debts in writing this book. I want to mention several in particular. The work of my teacher, the late Ludwig von Mises, was indispensable. And if there is a renaissance of the kind of society that combines freedom and community, the work of F. A. Hayek is the rock on which it will be built. The work of the late Wilhelm Röpke, especially his book *The Humane Economy*, is of great importance. Robert Nisbet's books, particularly *The Quest for Community* and *The Twilight of Authority*, seem to me to become more and more central as time passes. I have listed elsewhere a number of other exceptional books that touch on one or another of this book's principal themes. Irving Ferman contributed a pivotal concept: the tendency of a specialized society to lose the capacity to make the decisions on which its survival depends. Arthur Burns' Per Jacobsen lecture, "The Anguish of Central Banking," delivered in Belgrade in 1979, was of great value to me.

There are debts of another sort. Alex Saskas gave me two summers off from work. Kiril Sokoloff, Betty Friedan, Paul Manheim, Kirkpatrick Sale, Fred Sawyer, and George Harris were helpful at certain crucial intersections. Jack Kaplan gave me a boost that could not have been more perfectly timed.

I make my living as a writer, and much of this book is the unexpected result of projects assigned to me by various clients. Michael A. Taylor hired me to do a series of essays on the economy and worked closely with me on them. Don Austermann and John Cobbs of *Business Week* worked with me on a particularly useful and agreeable project. Lane Adams, Bill

Aramony, and Marvin Feldman all hired me for work which found its way into this book. I do not need to say that none of these would necessarily want to associate themselves with the book's propositions and probably some emphatically would not.

Helen Howard helped me with research. Working with her is always a great pleasure. Faith Sale, my editor, was wonderfully helpful, and I would be helpless without Donna Welensky.

Some Related Reading

Bailey, Stephen K., *Congress Makes a Law.* New York: Columbia University Press, 1950.

Bresciani-Turroni, Constantino, *The Economics of Inflation.* New York: Augustus M. Kelley, 1968.

Buchanan, James M., and Wagner, Richard E., *Democracy in Deficit.* New York: Academic Press, 1977.

Burns, Scott, *The Household Economy.* Boston: Beacon Press, 1977.

Cornuelle, Richard, *Reclaiming the American Dream.* New York: Random House, 1965.

Edel, Leon, *Bloomsbury: A House of Lions.* Philadelphia: J. B. Lippincott Company, 1979.

Etzioni, Amitai, *An Immodest Agenda—Rebuilding America before the 21st Century.* New York: McGraw-Hill, 1982.

Ferrara, Peter J., *Social Security: The Inherent Contradiction.* San Francisco: Cato Institute, 1980.

Friedrich, Otto, *Before the Deluge.* New York: Harper & Row, 1972.

Garraty, John A., *Unemployment in History.* New York: Harper & Row, 1978.

Griffiths, Brian, *Inflation: The Price of Prosperity.* London: Weidenfeld, 1976.

Hayek, F. A., *The Constitution of Liberty.* Chicago: University of Chicago Press, 1960.

———, *Studies in Philosophy, Politics and Economics.* London: Routledge & Kegan Paul, 1967.

Hoover, Herbert, *American Individualism.* New York: Garland Publishing, Inc., 1979.

Jacobs, Jane, *The Death and Life of Great American Cities.* New York: Random House, 1961.

Keynes, J. M., *Two Memoirs.* New York: Augustus M. Kelley, 1949.

Levin, Lowell S., and Idler, Ellen L., *The Hidden Health Care System.* Cambridge: Ballinger Publishing Company, 1981.

McCarthy, Rockne, *et al.*, *Society, State and Schools.* Grand Rapids: William B. Eerdmans Publishing Company, 1981.

Nielsen, Waldemar A., *The Endangered Sector.* New York: Columbia University Press, 1979.

Nisbet, Robert A., *The Quest for Community.* New York: Oxford University Press, 1953.

————, *Twilight of Authority.* New York: Oxford University Press, 1975.

Poole, Robert W., Jr., *Instead of Regulation.* Lexington: Lexington Books, 1982.

Röpke, Wilhelm, *A Humane Economy.* South Bend: Gateway Editions, 1960.

Rosen, Elliot A., *Hoover, Roosevelt, and the Brains Trust.* New York: Columbia University Press, 1977.

Schumpeter, Joseph A., *Ten Great Economists from Marx to Keynes.* New York: Oxford University Press, 1951.

Stein, Herbert, *The Fiscal Revolution in America.* Chicago: University of Chicago Press, 1969.

Wilson, Joan Hoff, *Herbert Hoover: Forgotten Progressive.* Boston: Little, Brown and Company, 1975.

Yeager, Leland B., *Experiences With Stopping Inflation.* Washington: American Enterprise Institute for Public Policy Research, 1981.

Index